HIKING & BIKING IN DuPAGE COUNTY, ILLINOIS

HIKING & BIKING IN DuPAGE COUNTY, ILLINOIS

by Jim Hochgesang

Editing and Nature Notes by Sheryl DeVore
Design by Melanie Lawson

A Roots & Wings Publication

Dedication

This book is dedicated to my wife, Sandy, who balanced many roles as mother, wife, homemaker, manuscript preparer, book distributor, and office administrator. Without her support, this book would not have been published.

Created by Sandy and Jim Hochgesang
Design by Melanie Lawson
Offset printing service by Rheitone, Inc.
Printed and bound by United Graphics, Inc.

Photography credits:
Front cover: John Kohout, Courtesy of The Morton Arboretum
Back Cover:
Black Swallowtail Butterfly by Brook McDonald
Fox Kits, Courtesy Forest Preserve District of DuPage County
Autumn Leaves by John Kohout, Courtesy of The Morton Arboretum
Illustration credit:
Page 93: Nancy Hart Stieber, Courtesy of The Morton Arboretum

ISBN 1-884721-01-X

Contents

Acknowledgments 7

Preface 8

Introduction 10

A Little History 16

County Map and Summary Table 20

Section 1 • The Illinois Prairie Path 26

Section 2 • The Great Western Trail 43

Section 3 • Pratt's Wayne Woods Forest Preserve 47

Section 4 • West Branch, DuPage River Greenway
(Mallard Lake, Hawk Hollow, West Branch
Forest Preserves, and Kline Creek Farm) 51

Section 5 • West Chicago Prairie Forest Preserve 56

Section 6 • West DuPage Woods Forest Preserve 59

Section 7 • The Wheaton EcoBelt 62

Section 8 • Blackwell Forest Preserve 67

Section 9 • Fermilab Bike Path and Nature Trails 73

Section 10 • Herrick Lake and Danada Forest Preserves .. 78

Section 11 • McDowell Grove Forest Preserve 84

Section 12 • Naperville Riverwalk, Naper Settlement, and Nearby Trails.................................87

Section 13 • Greene Valley Forest Preserve.......................90

Section 14 • The Morton Arboretum 93

Section 15 • Downer's Grove Area Preserves (Lyman Woods and Maple Grove)..................100

Section 16 • Willowbrook Wildlife Center.......................104

Section 17 • Churchill Woods Forest Preserve 107

Section 18 • Meacham Grove and Spring Creek Reservoir Forest Preserves 111

Section 19 • Northeastern Forest Preserve Trails (Cricket Creek, Salt Creek Park, and Wood Dale Grove Forest Preserves)................113

Section 20 • Salt Creek Greenway Trail and York Woods Forest Preserve.........................116

Section 21 • Oak Brook Bike Path....................................118

Section 22 • Fullersburg Woods Forest Preserve and Graue Mill 122

Section 23 • Waterfall Glen Forest Preserve 127

Section 24 • Greenway Interconnecting Trails................133

Section 25 • The Grand Illinois Trail...............................141

Appendices (Nearby Attractions, Bike Shops Calendar of Events, Organizations) 146

Bibliography 158

Comments/Order Form 159-160

Acknowledgments

We appreciate the support, input, and guidance of many professionals who reviewed our draft manuscript, provided source maps, and supplied information.

Sonya Baker, Naperville Park District
George Bellovics, Illinois Department of Conservation
Brian Charles, Fermilab
Bill Donnell, Fox Valley Park District
Jon Duerr, Kane County Forest Preserve District
Will Henniff, DuPage County Development Department,
    Planning Division
Alea Hashimoto, Brook McDonald, Jan Roehll, Forest Preserve
    District of DuPage County
Ken Kutska, Wheaton Park District
Joe Larkin, The Morton Arboretum
Richard Mariner, Northeastern Illinois Planning Commission
Jean and Paul Mooring, Illinois Prairie Path
Steve Plumb, Elmhurst Park District
Pat Saunders, Downers Grove Park District
Susan Stob, DuPage County Historical Museum
Tom Suhs, Oak Brook Parks Department
Chuck Tokarski, DuPage County Division of Transportation

A special thanks to the women and men involved in developing and maintaining the trails and pathways in DuPage and the adjoining counties.

Preface

Riding a bicycle past the glistening ocean, cross-country skiing at the foothills of a majestic mountain, hiking through a national forest. These activities can provide many hours of pleasure and exercise for the adventurous soul. But family and work obligations as well as time and money limitations can often make it difficult to get to those far away places.

My family and I have found a solution by exploring the forest preserves and natural areas much closer to home. We have learned that fascinating escapades await the hiker and biker right here in Chicagoland.

The discovery led me to take early retirement from corporate life in spring 1993 to write and publish hiking and biking guidebooks that would help people find these nearby adventures. On April 1, 1994, our fledgling company published *Hiking & Biking in Lake County, Illinois.* Thanks to the help and support of many people, the guidebook has been well received. Along the way on our publishing venture, we met and received letters from many people who told us they would enjoy a similar guidebook detailing the trails and bike paths of DuPage County. Trail users also told us they wanted more information on cross-country skiing and mountain bike trails.

We wrote this book with our fellow trail users in mind. Here we guide you through over 240 miles of trails and bike paths at 41 different DuPage County locations. For added enjoyment, we describe the flora, fauna, and terrain you will encounter as well as the unique history of this special county.

Exploring the many enjoyable trails and bike paths of DuPage County as research for this book was fun work. But somebody had to do it! We hope you find the trails as enjoyable and interesting as we have. Happy hiking, biking, and cross-country skiing.

Introduction

This book is for people who want to know where to find off-road trails and pathways in DuPage County, Illinois. It is also for those who want easy-to-use trail maps, want to know how the trails are interconnected, and are interested in knowing more about the environment, animals, and plants of each area.

We live in a hectic, stressful world. After spending long hours at the office, factory, home or store, we seek the outdoors to restore our energy. I am convinced that buried in our genes is some of the same wanderlust experienced by our ancestors, many generations removed. Although the need to roam was originally driven by the basic instinct to survive, it is now driven by the search for mental and physical well-being. Those wanting serenity can find it by taking trails and bike paths through DuPage County's woods, savannas, and prairies, and along its rivers, streams, lakes, and wetlands.

Fortunately, the county's forefathers had the foresight to save some of these areas for our enjoyment. In fact, DuPage County was the first place in the country where volunteers and local government agencies worked together to convert

Forest Preserve District of DuPage County

Herrick Lake Forest Preserve

an abandoned railroad right-of-way to an off-road trail system. The result was the Illinois Prairie Path, a renowned 55-mile trail system crossing DuPage County and stretching into Kane and Cook Counties. "Rails-to-Trails" has since become a significant national movement. The Illinois Prairie Path and the county's other trails are great places to bike, hike, run, and cross-country ski. The trails vary in difficulty and in length, offering opportunities for those of all ages with diverse experiences.

How to Use This Guide

You will find a DuPage County map identifying the trail locations on pages 20 and 21. Next, you will notice a summary table listing information such as trail length and surface for each site.

More detailed information on each site is provided in individual sections. You'll learn how to get to the site, where to park, what facilities and amenities are available such as bicycle racks, restrooms, and drinking fountains, and special information about plants and animals living in or visiting the area. Other attractions such as the

1890s Kline Creek Farm will be listed.

After the sections about the Illinois Prairie Path and Great Western Trail, the rest of the guidebook is organized following the river greenways. A greenway is a corridor of open land or water providing transportation for people and/or animals while preserving the natural environment. The county map on pages 20 and 21 shows the area's greenways. Many forest preserves and trails surround the east and west branches of the DuPage River and Salt Creek. Several new trails are being added along these greenways while existing ones are being connected.

DuPage County's forest preserves, except for certain areas, are open daily from one hour after sunrise to one hour after sunset. Nature programs and activities are offered year-round. Most preserves contain information signs near parking areas where you will find visitor's guides and individual brochures.

A quarterly publication, *The DuPage Conservationist,* provides updated information on what is happening at the DuPage preserves. The newsletter is free to DuPage County residents and costs $5.00 per year for non-residents. Call 708-790-4900.

Several other agencies that manage the sites also offer programs and activities, publish newsletters, and provide maps. You can find more detailed information on events, trail hours, and special exhibits in the sections describing each site.

The Illinois Prairie Path is the backbone of the DuPage County trail system. Coupled with the 35-mile Fox River Trail in Kane County, the Great Western Trail, and nearby forest preserve trails, an interconnected trail system of more than 140 miles exists for hiking and biking. In a few locations, a short on-road connection is required.

Hiking

DuPage County has walks to meet varying needs. Distances vary from less than 1 mile to 20 miles or more. For instance, you can take your young children for a short .6-mile walk along the nature trail at Willowbrook Wildlife Center with benches stationed on the way. The zealous backpacker can hike 20 miles or more on the Illinois Prairie Path.

Biking

Cyclists blaze their own trails from once around the block to across the country and back. DuPage County has many off-road trails for bicycling. Most of the parks and forest preserves in this guide provide multi-use trails open to bicyclists. We encourage those who can to use their bikes instead of cars to get to these areas. You'll get two great benefits: you'll save gas and get more exercise. Sometimes a short ride on a street or road is required to make the connection between two off-road trails; this guide tells you how. Also you will find a listing of nearby bike shops on page 151.

The Planning Division of the DuPage County Development Department has produced a helpful map showing major trails as well as roads and streets suitable for the beginning to the more-experienced bicyclist. Call 708-682-7230 to get a copy. This guide mentions roads identified on the bikeway map that connect from one off-road trail system to another. For example, Weisbrook Road connects the Aurora Branch of the Illinois Prairie Path and Herrick Lake Forest Preserve.

Mountain biking has recently become popular. Several of the trails described here have either mowed turf or packed earth surface which is sometimes bumpy or filled with roots and stones. I did ride the trails described on my road bike, but on several trails a mountain or hybrid bike would certainly have been more effective. Maybe one of my bike shop buddies will give me a good deal on a mountain bike if we sell enough guidebooks.

I enjoy a mixture of hiking and biking. A hike is contemplative, offering a chance to observe surrounding flora and fauna. A bike ride is more invigorating; you can cover more territory faster. I like to ride a trail and then return later to walk the areas I found most interesting.

Cross-Country Skiing

Until we moved to the Chicago area in 1983, I had never cross-country skied. The snowy winters of the mid 1980s gave me plenty of opportunities to learn. The DuPage County Forest Preserve District, the Division of Transportation, and most community parks departments encourage skiing their trails. Hikers and equestrians are asked to stay to the center of the trail leaving the outside for ski tracks.

Beginners may want to try sites that have mostly flat trails. Some examples include Pratt's Wayne Woods, Herrick Lake, or Greene Valley forest preserves. More experienced skiers might try the multi-use trail at Waterfall Glen which has a very hilly terrain and is patrolled by the Norsk Nordic Ski Patrol.

Rules of the Trail

The popularity of multi-use trails continues to grow. As a result, you may encounter bicyclists, runners, wheelchair users, hikers, equestrians, and rollerbladers. Please be courteous and considerate of others so that everyone can enjoy our DuPage County trails. Safety suggestions and regulations to protect the environment are described following this section. Please read them carefully.

Nearby Attractions, Calendar of Events, Organizations

In the appendices, you will find a list of attractions and area merchants furnished by the DuPage Convention and Visitors Bureau. A monthly calendar of events includes annual DuPage County activities. You will also find a listing of environmental, hiking, bicycling, and other related organizations. One example is the Conservation Foundation of DuPage County which works to preserve open lands in the county and promotes public access to these areas.

While we worked to find as many appropriate events and organization listings as we could, certainly some have been missed. Please notify us of any oversights for future issues of this guidebook. Our address is Roots & Wings, P. O. Box 167, Lake Forest, Illinois 60045.

Comments/Order Form

To improve future issues of *Hiking & Biking in DuPage County*, your comments would be very much appreciated. A form is on page 159. We'd also like to know if you'd be interested in future guidebooks. Page 160 contains an order form for those who want to purchase additional copies of this book or our first publication *Hiking & Biking in Lake County, Illinois*.

Rules of the Trail

- Deposit litter in proper receptacles.
- Leave nature as you find it for others to enjoy. Remain on the trail.
- Leash all pets. (Some preserves do not allow pets.)
- Be alert for cars or bicycles.
- Don't feed the wildlife.
- DuPage County forest preserves are open from one hour after sunrise to one hour after sunset daily. Hours of operation for other sites are shown in the sections describing each site.
- Don't wear earphones. You can't hear a bicyclist coming.
- Relax, have fun, and enjoy!
- Check for ticks when you're finished.

Specific for Bicyclists

- Wear a helmet.
- Be alert for loose gravel, debris, holes, or bumps on the trails.
- Take it easy with hikers of all ages on the trail.
- Ride in single file.
- Cautiously pass hikers on the left. Call out "passing on the left". But remember the hiker may be deaf or hard of hearing or may be wearing earphones.
- Keep both hands on your handle bars.
- Keep to designated bike trails in the forest preserves.
- See "Illinois Bicycle Rules" for additional safety information for on-road bicycling.

For your enjoyment

- Apply insect repellent before you go out depending on the season.
- Take water on long hikes or bike rides.

A Little History

An outdoor trip through DuPage County's preserves and natural areas can take you through millions of years of its vibrant history.

Bicycling past a high bluff overlooking the Des Plaines River at Waterfall Glen Forest Preserve in early spring, you can see the distant quarries of limestone deposits composed of fossilized sea creatures and plant life that lived there 400 million years ago.

Hike the Willowbrook Wildlife Center nature trail and you'll discover remnants of the last great Ice Age 20,000 years ago when massive boulders and large stones of granite were transported to the county from as far away as Ontario, Canada.

Inside the Fullersburg Forest Preserve's environmental theater, you can see the bones of a woolly mammoth that died 13,000 years ago, perhaps trapped in the mucky mire of a bog.

Near the Riverwalk in downtown Naperville, you can visit a

reconstruction of Fort Payne hurriedly built by soldiers during the Blackhawk War of 1832. And on the trail in Pioneer Park in Naperville, you'll find the millstones installed in 1834 by DuPage County's first settlers.

These DuPage County areas and many others offer the visitor glimpses to the past as far back as 500 million years ago when, like the rest of the Midwest, DuPage County was covered by the Silurian Sea, up until today when people are working to preserve their history and environment.

First Inhabitants

The first humans, the Paleo Indians, came to northern Illinois as the glaciers from the last Ice Age melted approximately 13,000 years ago. Their Asian ancestors had crossed a Siberian land bridge when ocean levels waned during the last glacial period. Little by little, succeeding generations worked their way southeast from what is today Alaska. As hunters of wild game and gatherers of seeds and berries, these nomadic people moved with the seasons to find sustenance.

When French fur traders and trappers came to the area in the 1660s, they encountered a confederacy of tribes led by the Illini. After a series of tribal wars, resulting partially from conflicts over the fur trade business with the French, the Illini were driven from the area.

The Potowatami predominated northeastern Illinois between the middle 1700s and 1830s. During this time period, according to traditional county history, a French fur trader, DuPage, traded goods with the Potowatami south of Naperville in what is now Will County. DuPage County and its major river are named after this early businessman.

In 1800, 6,000 Potowatami lived in 50 villages around the southern part of Lake Michigan from Milwaukee, Wisconsin, to St. Joseph, Michigan, according to Richard A. Thompson, author of *DuPage Roots*. In DuPage County, there were four major villages. One was near Oak Brook on Salt Creek, another near Naperville on the West Branch of the DuPage River, a third on the East Branch of the river in The Morton Arboretum, and the largest, also on the East Branch, in what is today Churchill Woods Forest Preserve.

The Potowatami planted corn, squash, peas, and beans along the river valleys near their villages. They fished the rivers and sent out hunting parties to track buffalo and deer on the prairies and savannas. But in the 1830s their lives changed.

Early Settlers

The first settlers, Bailey Hobson and his family, came to the DuPage County area from southern Indiana in March, 1831. By the end of the next year, 180 settlers had moved into the area. (Section 12 has more information on the Naper settlement.) The Potowatami mostly tolerated the newcomers and occasionally assisted them. In fact, during the Blackhawk War of 1832, Chief Aptakisic and others warned settlers of rampaging Sauk and Fox warriors in the area. After the war, the Treaty of Chicago ceded the territory to the newcomers. Chief Aptakisic and his tribe were relocated to the west side of the Missouri River.

The early settlers encountered a land quite different from the deep forests of the east. Instead, they walked through vast expanses of tall-grass prairie filled with 8-foot-tall big blue stem and many wildflowers of varying heights and colors. This great prairie extended from Iowa, Kansas, and Nebraska east to DuPage County and the Chicago area.

The settlers discovered beneath the prairies a fertile soil in which to raise crops and feed the burgeoning midwestern population. By the Civil War, DuPage County's population had skyrocketed to 15,000.

At the start of the "Roaring 20s", approximately 42,000 lived in the county. Even so, DuPage County was still mostly farm country. But a series of events beginning in the 1940s gradually and drastically changed the area. Argonne National Laboratory, the first American research institute for atomic fission, was built in 1947 in southeastern DuPage County. Fermilab, which houses the world's largest high energy particle accelerator, was built in 1973 west of Wheaton and Winfield. Manufacturing and research facilities also were built. Multi-lane highways including the Eisenhower Expressway, I-88, I-294, and I-55 made DuPage County easily accessible.

The county's population today is over 800,000 and increasing. During most of the 1980s, Naperville was the fastest growing community in the midwest. Rapid growth, of course, affected the environment. A trip through the county in the 1990s is quite different from what was experienced by the hunters, traders, and settlers 160 years ago. We can debate which lifestyle is better. I'll choose today, but like many other Chicagoland residents, I still cherish being out in the open lands.

Forest Preserves and Open Lands

Fortunately, DuPage County residents had the foresight to establish a forest preserve district in 1915. Today, the Forest Preserve District of DuPage County owns and manages more than 22,000 acres. A current goal is to restore the natural integrity to about 8,000 acres of the district's highest quality areas within the next decade through an unprecedented Natural Areas Management Program. The district is restoring prairies, wetlands, streams, and other important native ecosystems.

Community park districts, the Illinois Department of Conservation, and other governmental agencies and private organizations, are also expanding and restoring open lands. As you hike and bike DuPage County, you will notice much of this work in progress.

Some folks believe these open lands should be set aside with little or no human trespassers. I disagree. Trails open up beautiful natural areas to people of all ages, offering a link with our past as we explore native and restored prairies and wetlands. I believe that those who experience the joys of being out in nature will support initiatives to create and restore more open lands. Trail users, of course, must be responsible users, leaving the land as they find it for someone else to enjoy.

Enough preaching. On to the trails!

DuPage County Forest Preserves, Trails, and Pathways

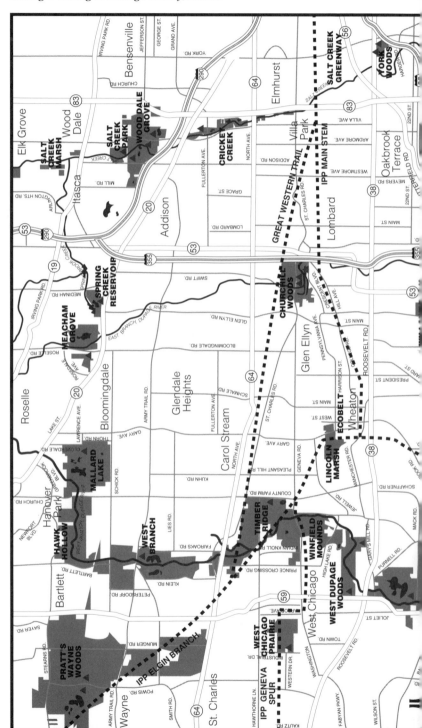

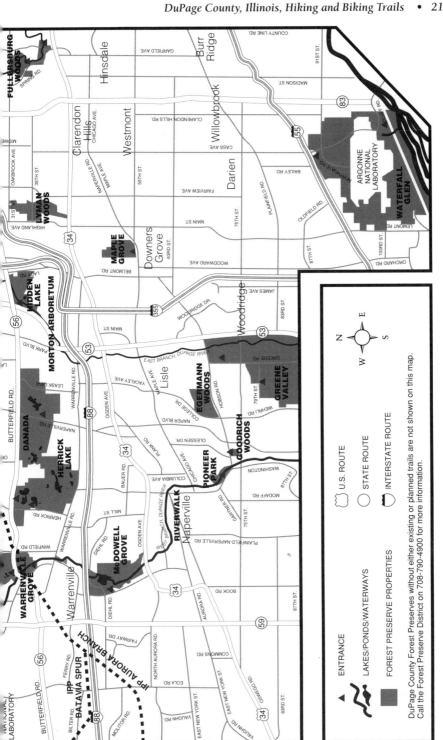

ENTRANCE

LAKES/PONDS/WATERWAYS

FOREST PRESERVE PROPERTIES

⬡ U.S. ROUTE

◯ STATE ROUTE

⬡ INTERSTATE ROUTE

DuPage County Forest Preserves without either existing or planned trails are not shown on this map. Call the Forest Preserve District on 708-790-4900 for more information.

Courtesy Forest Preserve District of DuPage County

DuPage County, Illinois, Hiking and Biking Trails

Park, Preserve, or Trail	Section	Miles–Hike	Bike	Surface	Author's Comments
Illinois Prairie Path	1	55*	55*	L (see note 1)	Main backbone trail system through DuPage County. Interconnects with many other trail systems. Geneva Spur to be completed in 1995. Cook County segment to be completed in 1996. Open to equestrians. (See note 2.)
Great Western Trail	2	11.4* (see note 3)	11.4*	L	Connects with IPP. Bridge planned over I-355. On-road detours extend trip to 12.2 miles. Open to equestrians.
Pratt's Wayne Woods Forest Preserve	3	9.7	9.1	M	Connects with Elgin Branch of IPP. Fat tires (i.e., mountain or hybrid bike) more effective on mowed turf surface. Loop trails open to equestrians.
West Branch, DuPage River Greenway	4				Greenway trail will eventually run from Mallard Lake to Naperville.
Mallard Lake FP		2.0	2.0	M	Mostly mowed turf path around the lake.
Hawk Hollow FP		4.1	4.1	M	Fat tires preferred. Open to equestrians.
West Branch FP		2.5	1.3	P	Hiking trail around the lake. Mowed turf trail along Klein Road open to equestrians.
Kline Creek Farm		.8*	.8*	L	New trail will be completed in 1995. Connects Great Western Trail and Elgin Branch of the IPP through Timber Ridge Forest Preserve.
West Chicago Prairie Forest Preserve	5	2.8	—	M	Connects with Geneva Spur of IPP. Open to hikers and cross-country skiers only.
West DuPage Woods Forest Preserve	6	3.8	3.8	M	1.3-mile Circle Trail on west side. 2.5-mile Elsen's Hill Circle Trail on east side. Open to equestrians.

Park, Preserve, or Trail	Section	Miles–Hike/Bike		Surface	Author's Comments
Wheaton EcoBelt	7				Will eventually connect Great Western Trail to Aurora Branch of the IPP. 2.8 miles of additional trails are currently planned.
Community Park		1.1	1.1	L, W	
Northside Park		1.5	1.5	M	
Lincoln Marsh		1.3	—	W	Many species of plants and animals reside in this natural habitat on the Elgin Branch of the IPP.
Atten Park		1.0	1.0	A	Connects to Aurora Branch of the IPP and to the FPD's Regional Trail.
Seven Gables Park		2.5	2.5	A	
Blackwell Forest Preserve	8	7.0*	7.0*	L, M	Trail mileage: Regional 3.3, Egret 1, Catbird .8, Bob-o-link 1.4, Nighthawk .5. Trails open to equestrians. .4-mile connection to the Aurora Branch of the IPP will be installed in 1995.
Fermilab Bike Path and Nature Trails	9	4.0 / 3.5	4.0 / —	A / W	Asphalt bike path runs from Kirk Road entrance on west side to Butterfield Road on east side. Connects with Batavia Spur and Aurora Branch of IPP. Woodchip hiking trail through prairie and woods.
Herrick Lake Preserve	10	6.5	6.5	L	Trail mileage: Regional 2.2, Lake 1, Meadowlark 1, Green Heron Forest 1.9, Bluebird .4. Connects with Danada Regional Trail and sidewalk connection to Aurora Branch of IPP. Trails open to equestrians.
Danada Forest Preserve	10	2.9	2.9	L	2-mile Regional Trail continues through Herrick Lake Forest Preserve .9-mile Parson's Grove nature trail. Regional Trail open to equestrians.
McDowell Grove	11	5.6*	5.6*	M	Be cautious on dirt hiking trails along the river. 3.7-mile Forest Preserve limestone trail to be installed in 1995 along the DuPage River. Trails open to equestrians.

Park, Preserve, or Trail	Section	Miles–Hike/Bike		Surface	Author's Comments
Naperville Riverwalk and Nearby Trails	12				
Riverwalk		2.5	—	B	Hiking only on Riverwalk. Near Naper Settlement.
Pioneer Park		1.0	—	P	
Goodrich Woods		.5	—	P	
Egerman Woods		.5	—	M	
Greene Valley Forest Preserve	13	6.2*	6.2*	M	1-mile woodchip Tricky Tree Trail in youth campground area for hiking only. Multi-use trails open to equestrians. 2.4-mile limestone trail along the DuPage River to be installed by 1996.
The Morton Arboretum	14	25	—	W, L, A	Several trails through mature woodlands with rolling hills. 10-mile auto road with parking at 27 sites. Excellent fall foliage. Hiking only.
Downers Grove Area Preserves	15				
Lyman Woods		1.3	—	M, P	Hiking only.
Maple Grove FP		1.0	1.0	P	Great place for fall foliage color.
Willowbrook Wildlife Center	16	.6	—	L	Nice spot for a short hike with kids and a visit with the animals.
Churchill Woods Forest Preserve	17	2.3	2.3	M, L	Site of largest Potowatami village in the county. 2-mile main trail. .3-mile cutback trail. Connects with Great Western Trail north of prairie.
Meacham Grove Forest Preserve	18	1.0	—	P	Great place for spring wildflowers and fall color.
Spring Creek Forest Preserve	18	1.2	1.2	A	Good place to take kids learning to ride a bike.

Park, Preserve, or Trail	Section	Miles–Hike/Bike		Surface	Author's Comments
Northeastern Forest Preserve Trails	19				
Salt Creek FP		1.7	1.7	M	
Wood Dale Grove FP		1.2	1.2	A	Trail around the lake and through woods.
Cricket Creek FP		1.4	1.4	L	Recently opened 1.4-mile trail encircles fishing ponds near Salt Creek.
Salt Creek Greenway Trail	20	1.1	1.1	W	Mostly woodchip trail connects with IPP Main Stem via Rex Blvd.
Eldridge Park		1.0	1.0	A	Connects to Salt Creek Greenway Trail.
York Woods FP		1.2	1.2	A	Forest Preserve District's first preserve, purchased in 1921.
Oak Brook Bike Path	21	10	10	A, L	10 miles of off-road trails & bike paths plus 5 miles of on-road bike route.
Fullersburg Woods Forest Preserve	22	4.8	3.8	L	A.3-mile wildflower trail open to hikers only. Nature trail open to hikers and cross-country skiers. 3.3 miles open to equestrians.
Waterfall Glen Forest Preserve	23	9.5*	9.5*	L, M	9.5-mile multi-use main trail. 8-foot wide fire lanes & mowed turf open to bicycling. Side trails open to hikers only. Multi-use trails open to equestrians.
Nearby interconnecting trails	24				Major trail systems in nearby counties interconnect with DuPage County trails. (See note 4).
Fox River Trail		35	35	A	Connects with IPP at four locations. Runs from Aurora to Algonquin.
Prairie Trail-South		4.7*	4.7*	A	This Rails-to-Trails conversion connects via Fox River Trail.

Note 1.) Surface designations: L- crushed limestone, A- asphalt, B- brick, M- mowed turf, P-packed earth, W- woodchip. Typically a mountain or hybrid bike is more effective on a mowed turf or woodchip trail

Note 2.) Cross-country skiing in the winter is welcomed except for those trails designated hiking only.

Note 3.) *Signifies additional trails under construction or planned.

Note 4.) Other major trail systems in adjoining counties will interconnect with DuPage County trails in the future. Some examples are Cook County's Des Plaines River Trail, Ned Brown Forest Preserve trail, Salt Creek Bike Path, and the Centennial Trail. In Kane County, the Great Western Trail and the Virgil Gilman Trail will connect with the Fox River Trail. In Will County, the Illinois and Michigan Canal State Trail and Centennial Trail will connect via the DuPage County portion of the Centennial Trail.

The Illinois Prairie Path

Perhaps the best way to see DuPage County is to bike or hike the Illinois Prairie Path (IPP). Built on an abandoned railroad right-of-way, this 55-mile trail system runs as a single pathway west from the community of Maywood in Cook County across eastern DuPage County to the IPP focal point in Wheaton. From the Wheaton trailhead, a northwest branch leads to Elgin and a southwest trail runs to Aurora in Kane County. Spurs off the two westbound branches run to Geneva on the northwest route and Batavia on the southwest. Shaped like a sideways rake, the IPP serves as the backbone and connects with many other trails in the area. As a result, hikers and bikers have access to the most extensive interconnected trail system in the Chicago area. Even better is that projects are underway or planned to significantly expand this network of trails.

The IPP was built on the roadbed of the Chicago, Aurora, and Elgin Railroad (C.A.& E.), an electric commuter line that served the western suburbs for 56 years from 1902 to

1957. Called the "Great Third Rail", the railroad prospered for many years with fast, low-cost service. Back then the competition was steam-driven, soot-producing trains. But improved highways and more personal ownership of automobiles brought a more powerful new competition. The railroad then suffered a series of financial difficulties resulting in termination of passenger service on July 3, 1957. Freight trains continued to operate a few more years until the C.A.& E. abandoned the line entirely in June, 1961.

A naturalist at The Morton Arboretum, May Theilgaard Watts, suggested turning the abandoned roadbed into a path system where people could walk and bicycle through natural areas. Watts, a teacher and an author of books and poems detailing the Chicago area, was a well-respected environmentalist long before it was popular to be so. A poem she wrote in the early 1900s calling grass the grave site of former native flora and fauna foreshadows today's movement toward naturalized plantings. Her visionary skills combined with the hard work of many other dedicated volunteers as well as local publicity helped carve the future for the IPP. With the help of many supporters, The Illinois Prairie Path was formed in 1965 as a non-profit organization. Right-of-way was leased from DuPage County and the Illinois Department of Conservation in Kane and Cook Counties. The IPP became the first of many "rails-to-trails" conversions throughout the country and is recognized nationally.

How to get there:

You will find numerous places to park near the IPP. Probably the best place for a first-timer is at the Wheaton trailhead. Take Route 53 or I-355 from the north or south. From I-355, exit Roosevelt Road west for 3.3 miles to Carlton Avenue. Head north on Carlton for .3 mile to the IPP trailhead in Volunteer Park at the intersection of Carlton and Liberty Drive. You can park at the parking garage to the right for just $1 daily during the week and free on weekends. You will also find metered parking the first block south on Carlton. Farther south is FREE four-hour parking on Carlton north of Roosevelt. Additional parking locations along the IPP are described at the end of this section.

You will find a display case with information about the IPP as well as a free map and a water fountain at Volunteer Park. The name of the starting point is very appropriate given the literally thousands of volunteers who have contributed their time and talents to make the IPP a premier trail system.

The DuPage and Kane sections, encompassing more than 50 miles of the IPP, are very well maintained and delightful places to hike or bike. That is currently not the case for much of the 4.5-mile Cook County section. Fortunately, the Illinois Department of Conservation plans to complete improvements in the second half of 1996.

In DuPage County, the trail is 10 feet wide with a crushed limestone surface. In Kane County, the surface is primarily asphalt. The IPP is not a place to try to set a landspeed record. Some of the street crossings along the way are in quiet residential areas; others are in busy downtown areas. Be sure to obey the stop signs. At most crossings, there is a metal post in the center of the trail as well as two posts near the sides of the path to keep out motorized vehicles. If you are biking, go slow as you pass through. Take your time and enjoy the parks, forest preserves, communities and other points of interest along the way. A map on pages 30 and 31 displays the branches and spurs of the IPP as well as the major roads and streets.

The Illinois Prairie Path is open for cross-country skiing in winter. However, areas with many street crossings, such as most of the Main Stem, are not conducive to extended skiing.

Main Stem (Eastern Branch)

The eastern Main Stem section consists of 15 miles of trail from downtown Wheaton to First Avenue in Maywood. Assuming you parked near the Wheaton trailhead at Volunteer Park as described above, head east on the wide sidewalk on the north side of Liberty Drive to West Street. The off-road trail starts at West Street near the Wheaton Metra station. As you pass through Founder's Park, observe the rock monument with the inscription " 'Footpaths are defended with spirit by their users.' May Theilgaard Watts." After several street crossings, the surrounding environment quickly changes from the downtown business area to a quieter residential neighborhood (1.4 miles out). Honeysuckle bushes and trees on both sides of the trail provide a peaceful shady passage. On your right 1.8 miles out is Hoffman Park with picnic tables, playground equipment, ball fields, and a water fountain. (Mileage distances shown for both the branches and the spurs are always from the trailhead at Volunteer Park in Wheaton.)

After 2.9 miles, you will cross Main Street in Glen Ellyn and proceed through the Metra train station area. Prairie Path Park in downtown Glen Ellyn has benches, a water fountain, and a bike rack. East of downtown watch out for a fairly steep hill on both sides of the Taylor Avenue crossing. Here you will pass a small prairie restoration area planted in 1975 by Glenbard West High School students. A bridge crosses over the East Branch of the DuPage River at 4.6 miles. Twice swept away by the 100-year floods of 1972, then later burned by vandals, the bridge is a testimonial to the persistence and dedication of the volunteers and professionals who maintain the IPP.

At 4.6 miles out, you will pass over I-355 on a huge bridge built for IPP users. The community of Lombard follows with another main street crossing at 5.4 miles out. As you leave the downtown area, the mature trees provide welcome shade. At 7 miles out, you will enter Villa Park. Streetlights line the path through a long linear park. Playgrounds, a water fountain, and picnic tables are available. At 8 miles, you will pass the Villa Park Historical Society Museum and IPP Visitors Center. Housed in the former train station for the long departed electric line, the museum displays memorabilia from the defunct railroad and the Wander Corporation (maker of Ovaltine). Hours are Tuesday-Friday 2-6 p.m. and Saturday-Sunday 10 a.m. to 4 p.m. A bike rack, water fountain, and restroom are available. History buffs will enjoy stopping for a visit. Two short blocks north of the museum on Villa Avenue is the eastern trailhead for the Great Western Trail (Section 2).

At 8.3 miles out, you will enter the city of Elmhurst. Two bridge crossings take the trail user over first Route 83 and then Salt Creek. There are plans, though not yet funded, to develop an extensive 38-mile Salt Creek Greenway Trail extending north to the Ned Brown Forest Preserve and southeast to the 20-mile Centennial Trail currently under development. (See Section 24 for more information.)

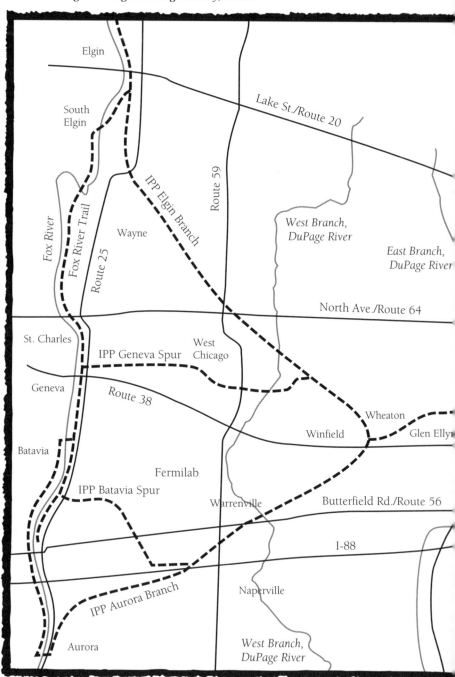

The Illinois Prairie Path

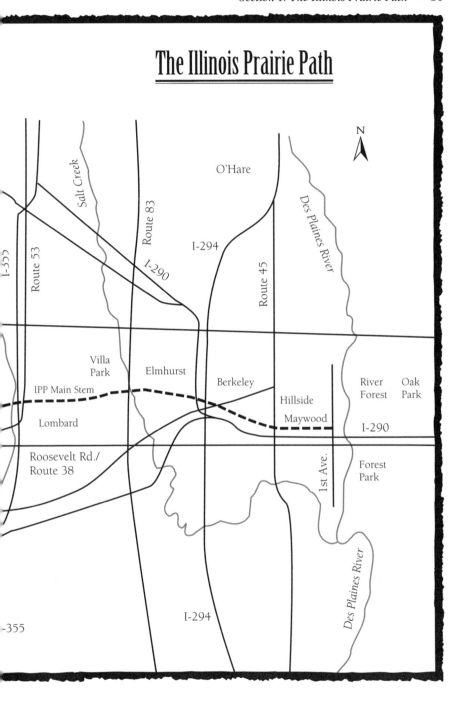

In Elmhurst, the community park district has restored 6 acres of tallgrass prairie from Salt Creek to Spring Road along the IPP. At the Berkley Street intersection, you will discover an interpretive garden labeling the native prairie plants our ancestors discovered hundreds of years ago. Blooming in mid-summer are purple coneflowers with their large lavender drooping petals. You will also find the lavender-hued blazing star which blooms in an unusual manner, from the top down. The more careful observer might discover a less common prairie species, the rattlesnake master. This plant has tight, round spiny balls upon which miniature white flowers bloom.

Many trees incompatible with the prairie environment were removed from this area. While I love wooded trails, I have also come to appreciate and enjoy the diversity of plant and animal life and the subtle changing colors found in a prairie. As you hike or bike your way through the IPP communities, you will find several prairie restoration projects. The Elmhurst Great Western and the West Chicago Prairie are the largest. Water fountains and picnic tables are available at Wild Meadows Trace Park at Spring Avenue 9 miles out and also farther east.

Leaving Elmhurst (at 10.6 miles), the IPP runs under I-294 entering Cook County. The path under the bridge is bumpy. The trail continues through the Cook County community of Berkeley. A park with picnic tables, drinking water, restrooms and a bike rack is east of the bridge. The IPP temporarily ends in Hillside shortly after a bridge over Wolf Road at 11.5 miles out. I suggest turning around at the small electric substation on the trail. Farther east are 2.5 miles of path from Mannheim Road in Bellwood to 1st Avenue in Maywood. However, the trail surface is rough in spots due to water main repair. Also, there were obstructions on the path when I visited. The Illinois Department of Conservation plans to improve the Cook County section with construction slated for the second half of 1996. Cook County agencies plan to extend the path .5 mile east across the Des Plaines River to the Chicago Transit Authority station at Des Plaines Avenue in Forest Park. Also, a multi-use trail is envisioned to head south along the river to Summit as part of the proposed Grand Illinois Trail (Section 25).

The Illinois Prairie Path

Cyclists on the Illinois Prairie Path at Volunteer Park.

Elgin Branch

From the Wheaton trailhead at Liberty Drive and Carlton Avenue, take the pathway heading north over Volunteer Bridge. In 1983, volunteers, with their own hands, restored the 160-foot-long iron truss bridge and added three 70-foot spans to cross over two city streets, a small park, as well as the railroad tracks. This portion of the IPP runs 15.7 miles to Elgin where it connects with the Fox River Trail (more on that later). After crossing the bridge, the path soon enters a tunnel of trees. At .7 mile out is a good spot to observe the Lincoln Marsh Natural Area. An observation platform to your left has benches as well as stairs down to a platform by the water's edge. You will see Canada geese and other migrating waterfowl such as bufflehead ducks and mallards in spring and fall stopping to rest before heading to their wintering or breeding grounds. A checklist of birds seen in the Lincoln Marsh is available from the Friends of Lincoln Marsh. With a long straight stretch of trail, this is a very picturesque place. A short distance farther northwest, a wooden boardwalk leads to a woodchip nature trail through the marsh. This trail is for hikers only. Bicyclists can lock up at the bottom of the boardwalk. A bit farther a limestone side trail for bicyclists as well as hikers also leads through the natural area. Lincoln Marsh is part of the Wheaton EcoBelt. (See Section 7 for more information.)

Back on the IPP, there are street crossings at Jewell Road and Pleasant Hill Road. At the County Farm/Geneva Road intersection (2.5 miles out), the IPP splits in two. The Geneva Spur, when completed in 1995, will head west along the south side of Geneva Road (see Page 36). The Elgin Branch continues in the northwest quadrant of the intersection. There you will find free IPP maps and a bench, as well as a small parking area. Here the IPP enters the Timber Ridge Forest Preserve. Also in 1995, a new .8-mile multi-use trail will be completed through Timber Ridge heading north on the west side of County Farm Road to Kline Creek Farm (Section 4) and the Great Western Trail. At 2.9 miles out, you will cross a bridge over Kline Creek. This is a very peaceful, shady area with marshland along the trail. A bridge crosses over the West Branch of the DuPage River at 4.2 miles.

At 4.7 miles out, you will come to Prince Crossing Road. Note the old brick building after you cross the street. This was an electric substation and ticket office for the C.A.& E. railroad. At 5 miles is a slough where beavers have done their work. On my visits here in 1994, cyclists had to port their bikes up a 20-foot climb to an intersection with the Great Western Trail (Section 2). Across the trail was a somewhat hidden path down the hill to continue heading northwest on the Elgin Branch. By the time you read this, an improved crossing, scheduled for 1995, should be completed.

Farther west a North Avenue underpass simplifies the crossing of this very busy road. At Route 59 (approximately 6.4 miles out), a new pedestrian bridge was opened in fall, 1994. Northeast is St. Andrew's Golf Course. West of Route 59, the path is again shady with patches of sunlight sprinkled on the trail through the towering trees. At 8.7 miles, there is a steep downhill grade to a railroad track crossing. There are roots and stumps on the narrow trail. Walk your bike through this area.

There is a portable toilet and bench at the Army Trail Road crossing at 9.1 miles. The entrance to Pratt's Wayne Woods Forest Preserve (Section 3) is .7 mile to the right on the Powis Road crossing at 9.2 miles out. This is an excellent place to visit or park when you're hiking or biking the Elgin Branch of the IPP.

Back on the IPP, the path leads through marshes along the border of the forest preserve and then crosses over Norton Creek at 9.8 miles. Here the path enters into Pratt's Wayne Woods. The trail leads first through forest, then wetlands. Brewster Creek forms a pond in the marsh to the east. A bench along the trail is a good resting spot with a scenic view of the marsh. Farther northwest on the IPP, a forest preserve trail heads east to a large equestrian jump area. Leaving the forest preserve, the trail enters Kane County at 11 miles out at Dunham Road. Bridges provide a safe crossing over the Chicago Central and Pacific (C.C.P.) railroad tracks and Route 25.

Proceeding farther into Kane County, the woods give way to farmland. The Valley Model Railroad Association now occupies the old brick Clintonville Station that served as a substation for the electric commuter line.

At 14 miles out, the path intersects with the Fox River Trail south of Elgin. On a sunny May day, two other bikers and I watched four adult Canada geese and at least 25 goslings meander along the river. The adults guarded the perimeter as the entourage quietly floated by. Unfortunately, I had no camera! The Fox River Trail heads south to Aurora and north to the McHenry County Prairie Trail which runs to Crystal Lake. (See Section 24.) The round-trip distance back to the Wheaton trailhead is 28 miles from this point.

The Illinois Prairie Path

Running on the Illinois Prairie Path.

The IPP and the Fox River Trail coexist on the same pathway consisting of both off-trail and on-street routes for another 1.7 miles heading north to Prairie Street in Elgin. If you continue north, be very cautious at the railroad crossing on Raymond Street. At 15.3 miles out, you will come to the new riverboat gambling casino at National Street. The path continues north under a covered walkway. There is an air pump if your tires are low and a bike rack if you are feeling lucky. Unless you intend to continue on the Fox River Trail, turn back here. The northern IPP trailhead is at Prairie Street north of the riverboat. Follow the bike path signs through Elgin to continue north on the Fox River Trail.

Geneva Spur

The newest member of the IPP family of trail branches and spurs is the path to Geneva. In 1995, the DuPage County Division of Transportation will open 3.7 miles of crushed limestone trail from the southwest corner of the intersection of County Farm Road and Geneva Road in Winfield to Reed Keppler Park in West Chicago. The trail will run through Winfield Mounds Forest Preserve with a bridge crossing over the West Branch of the DuPage River. At Reed Keppler Park, 6.7 miles out from the Wheaton trailhead, the new path connects with the existing trail that leads to the Fox River Trail in Geneva.

West of Reed Keppler Park, the IPP crosses over seven railroad tracks leading to the Metra maintenance station just outside West Chicago. Thanks to a very long bridge built for the trail users, it's an easy crossing. The path here is through mostly open prairie and marshland. Approximately 7 miles out, there are four very narrow (and easy to miss) pathways on the south side of the IPP that lead into the West Chicago Prairie Forest Preserve (Section 5). The prairie trails are open to hikers only.

Farther west the IPP runs between the DuPage County Airport to the north and the new Prairie Landing public golf course to the south. There are no trees here to provide shade plus there are no water fountains between Reed Keppler Park and the Fox River in Geneva, so bring water. Cornfields surround the path west of the golf course as it enters Kane County. There are only five street crossings over the 5 miles from West Chicago to Geneva. Unfortunately one at Kirk Road has extremely heavy traffic and high curbs. Be very careful here. I would not recommend crossing with young children. A bridge or a stoplight is definitely needed. At East Side Drive, the trail runs north (right) on a wide sidewalk to High Street. Head west on High Street for a short distance. The off-road path resumes to the right and enters Good Templar Park. The pathway crosses over a steep ravine on a bridge and proceeds to a switch-back ramp down to Route 25. Cross Route 25 with caution.

Across the road, the Geneva Spur meets the Fox River Trail. A short distance south in Bennett Park, picnic tables and parking are available. The Fox River Trail runs north and south through the park on the east side of the river. The Geneva Spur spans 8.6 miles from Winfield to Geneva.

Aurora Branch

From the northern trailhead at Volunteer Park in Wheaton, take the limestone path along Carlton Avenue .3 mile south to Roosevelt Road.

Use the pedestrian button to get a green light. The off-road trail begins south of Roosevelt Road. The mile markers are based on starting at the main IPP trailhead at Liberty and Carlton so we'll use that starting point to avoid confusion.

The path leads through quiet neighborhoods with trees lining the IPP. The first side trail to your left (.4 mile out) leads to Prairie Path Park, a secluded spot in the woods with water fountain, picnic tables, and playground equipment but no restrooms. At 1.5 miles out be careful crossing Orchard Road, a busy street where cars come fast around a curve in the road. At 2.5 miles out, there is a crossing at Weisbrook Road. The IPP continues straight ahead across the street. The path right takes you to Wheaton's Atten Park with 1-mile asphalt trail, playground, drinking water, picnic tables, restrooms, and a secluded wooded area with a short path. The sidewalk on the west side of Weisbrook Road in front of Wheaton-Warrenville South High School heads south .5 mile to the intersection with Butterfield Road. Diagonally across the street is a trail entrance to Herrick Lake Forest Preserve (Section 10).

Continuing southwest on the IPP from Weisbrook Road, the trail is tree-lined and peaceful unless you have a near head-on collision with a "Kamikaze" squirrel as I almost did. Three and one-half miles out is Saint James Farm, a large horse farm. A tunnel crosses under Butterfield Road at 3.7 miles out. The surrounding countryside is now mostly farmland as the path parallels Butterfield Road/Route 56 for a bit. At 4.1 miles, the IPP crosses Winfield Road at the stop light. Note the pedestrian button. The Blackwell Forest Preserve entrance is .4 mile west on Butterfield Road. A connecting path is planned for completion in 1995 as part of the Regional Trail. (See Section 8.) The IPP heads south along Winfield Road for about 300 feet and then west through Warrenville Grove Forest Preserve. This is a peaceful woodsy area. A bridge crosses over the West Branch of the DuPage River. As you enter Warrenville, the sidewalk on the west side of Batavia Road is the beginning of the bike path which heads north into Fermilab (Section 9).

After crossing Batavia Road at 4.9 miles on the IPP, you will come to the Warrenville municipal building—another former C.A.& E.

train station. A water fountain, picnic tables, a portable toilet, and a bike rack are available. Soft drinks and coffee can be found at a nearby coffee house.

For a side trip, the entrance to Warrenville Grove Forest Preserve is .4 mile south on Batavia Road. You will find a sidewalk most of the way. While there are no established trails at this preserve, you might enjoy the waterfall at the river dam or walking the short dirt paths through the woods.

Back on the IPP, there is a small park (Sesquicentennial) at 5.5 miles with picnic tables, a drinking fountain, and a restroom. Tall trees border the path. At 6.3 miles, there is a single lane tunnel under Route 59. Walk your bike through the underpass. The Batavia Spur heads off to the right at 7.3 miles out. (See page 40.)

The Aurora Branch continues south with an underpass beneath I-88. At 8.2 miles, you will need to carry your bike over the Elgin, Joliet, and Eastern (E.J.& E.) railroad tracks. Power lines run along the trail for about 1.5 miles. Farther west, Eola Road and Farnsworth Road crossings are quite busy. Eola Road will be widened to four lanes. The project will start in 1995 and will include a bridge for the Aurora Branch and a tunnel for the Batavia Spur. At 11 miles, you will cross over Indian Creek. The trail is tree-lined for a bit before entering the outskirts of Aurora. At 12 miles is the Indian Trail Road crossing as you enter a residential area. At 12.5 miles, follow the bike path sign onto Hankes Road. A very busy Route 25 crossing is at 12.6 miles. A stoplight is definitely needed here. Use caution when crossing. The IPP continues across the road and down a hill into a community park. The IPP parking area and southwestern trailhead is 13 miles out just north of Illinois Avenue and east of the Fox River. The IPP and the Fox River Trail are contiguous from Illinois Avenue to New York Street where you will find a riverwalk and another riverboat casino. If you are interested in continuing north on the Fox River Trail, cross over the river on Illinois Avenue to McCollough Park on the west bank. The Fox River southern trailhead is located there. A bike rack, telephone, water fountain, parking, and restrooms are available at the community center in McCollough Park.

Batavia Spur

You will find practically no trees here, mostly a lot of farm land. If you need a break, there's a bench where you can sit and listen to the corn grow. This fertile land was originally part of the great prairie. You will have to carry your bike across another railroad track here. Electric power lines follow the path for a distance. Two miles from the start of the spur, the pathway is again tree-lined and passes by two ponds. At 9.8 miles, the path enters Kane County. White and pink honeysuckles and wildflowers border the trail. At 11.2 miles out from the Wheaton trailhead, the path crosses very busy Kirk Road just west of Fermilab. I finally got across after a long wait. I don't recommend crossing with small children. The good news is that an overpass will be installed in 1995. This is a good example of the on-going improvements on the IPP. If you take the asphalt path on the west side of Kirk Road heading north for .8 mile, you can access the Fermilab bike path at Pine Street.

West of Fermilab, the Kane County trail is asphalt-surfaced and tree-lined. After crossing Raddant and Hart Roads, you will come to the intersection with the Fox River Trail at 13.5 miles out from the start in Wheaton. Note the sign at the Y intersection of the trail: "East to Fermilab, Wheaton 13.5 miles. South to N. Aurora/Aurora. North to Batavia, Geneva, St. Charles, Elgin." A short distance to the south at Glenwood Park Forest Preserve, you will find a water fountain, picnic tables, parking, and restrooms. One mile farther south on the Fox River Trail is the Red Oak Nature Center. The Batavia Spur continues north for another 1.1 miles contiguous with the Fox River Trail. The western trailhead is at the foot of the stairs leading up to Wilson Street in downtown Batavia.

Parking

The Illinois Prairie Path organization has identified the following parking locations:

MAIN STEM

There is public parking near the IPP in all the villages and cities along the Main Stem. Most of it is metered parking or leased parking for commuters, but some free parking exists. In Cook County the IPP runs generally through residential areas where you can find free parking along adjacent or cross streets. On weekends most leased parking spaces can almost always be used on Sundays without feeding the meters.

Parking is free at the following sites.

Elmhurst: (1) Parking lot east of York Road between Vallette Street and the IPP. Enter from Vallette. (2) Pioneer Park at the east end of Prairie Path Lane where the IPP crosses the Chicago Central and Pacific Railroad. (3) West of Spring Road north of IPP. (4) Prairie Path Lane south of the IPP and west of Berkeley.

Villa Park: (1) Parking lot west of Villa Avenue on Central Boulevard. Be sure to visit the Illinois Prairie Path Visitor Center in the Villa Park Historical Museum. (2) West of Ardmore Avenue on Central and Park Boulevards.

Lombard: (1) Parking lot west of Westmore Avenue. (2) Along Broadway on both sides of the IPP.

Glen Ellyn: (1) Hill Avenue near the Glen Oak Country Club between Glen Ellyn and Lombard. (2) Along Walnut Street from Lowell to Taylor. (3) The western end of Duane Street. Enter the IPP from Danby Park.

Wheaton: Elmer J. Hoffman Park. Enter north from Hill Avenue on Prospect Street, one block east of the Northwestern railroad crossing.

West of Wheaton there is room for one or two cars where most roads cross the IPP. Here we list streets where more extensive parking is available near the path.

ELGIN BRANCH

(1) In Wheaton along Lincoln and Western Avenues near the IPP. (2) Both sides of Jewell Road. (3) On the northwest corner of County Farm and Geneva Roads. (4) Along the abandoned Frontage Road north of North Avenue and west of the IPP. Enter from North Avenue. (5) Both sides of Army Trail Road, Wayne. (6) Clintonville Station. (7) Raymond Street, Elgin.

AURORA BRANCH

(1) Center Street, Wheaton. (2) West side of Winfield Road.
(3) South of the IPP and east of Batavia Road, Warrenville. (4) Large
parking lots south of the IPP near the Warrenville city hall and the
public library. Turn west from Batavia Road one block south of the
IPP, go one block, then turn right (north) to lots. (5) West side of Eola
Road. (6) West side of Farnsworth Avenue in Aurora. (7) McCullough
Park east of the Fox River in Aurora. Enter from Illinois Avenue.
(8) The Burlington Northern commuter parking lot on the east side
of Illinois Route 25 in Aurora.

BATAVIA SPUR

(1) Bilter Road. (2) Glenwood Park Forest Preserve, Batavia. The
entrance to the preserve is on the west side of Illinois Route 25 just
south of the Batavia Spur.

GENEVA SPUR

(1) County Farm and Geneva Roads. (2) Reed-Keppler Park, National Street, West Chicago. (3) Bennett Park on the east side of the
Fox River in Geneva. Enter from Illinois Route 25.

The DuPage County portion of the IPP is maintained by the Du-
Page County Division of Transportation. For further information, call
708-682-7318. In Kane County, the Kane County Forest Preserve
District maintains the spurs and the Elgin Branch. The telephone
number is 708-232-5980. The Aurora Branch is maintained by the
Fox Valley Park District at 708-897-0516. The Cook County section
is maintained by the Illinois Department of Conservation at 312-917-
2070.

If you are interested in becoming a member of The Illinois Prairie
Path organization, you can obtain a membership application by
writing to The Illinois Prairie Path, P. O. Box 1086, Wheaton, IL
60189 or calling 708-752-0120. Members receive a quarterly newsletter and a large IPP map. Your contribution will help maintain and
improve the Illinois Prairie Path.

The Great Western Trail

Another major rails-to-trails conversion is the Great Western Trail built on the right-of-way of the defunct Great Western Railroad. An 18-mile section in Kane County starts in St. Charles and heads west to Sycamore in DeKalb County. An 11.4-mile DuPage County Great Western Trail was opened in 1992. The western trailhead is at an intersection with the IPP near Timber Ridge Forest Preserve .3 mile west of Prince Crossing Road and south of North Avenue/Route 64. (See Section 1.) The 10-foot wide crushed limestone trail heads east on an elevated road bed through a forest preserve, farmland, residential neighborhoods, and some business and industrial areas. The eastern trailhead is in downtown Villa Park. There are long stretches without access to drinking fountains, so bring water during hot weather.

How to get there:

There is no direct road access at the western trailhead today. Take the Elgin Branch of the IPP on bike or foot to get to the western trailhead. Near the

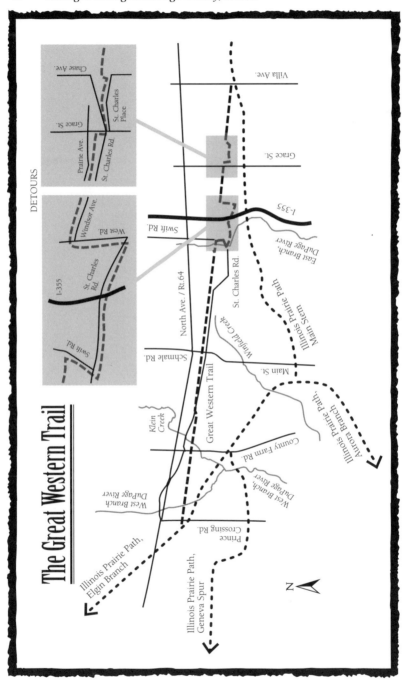

eastern trailhead at Villa Avenue in Villa Park, there is ample parking available in the downtown area. In between, a good place to leave your car is the Churchill Woods Forest Preserve (Section 17). The DuPage County Division of Transportation (DOT) will add parking areas as part of future trail projects.

Heading east from the western trailhead, through Timber Ridge Forest Preserve, there are wildflowers, wetlands, and woods along the trail. Much of the way, there are also electric power lines overhead. And once you've seen one electric power tower, you've seen them all. There are a few street crossings with high curbs so be sure to come to a complete stop. The DOT will be removing these high curbs as funding permits. In the first mile, you'll cross bridges over the West Branch of the DuPage River and Kline Creek. An .8-mile multi-use trail will be opened in 1995 from the Great Western Trail south through Timber Ridge Forest Preserve to Kline Creek Farm (Section 4) and from there, south to the Elgin Branch of the IPP near County Farm Road. Farther west you'll cross four-lane County Farm Road at 2.1 miles out and Schmale Road at 4.8 miles. Continuing on brings you to a bridge over the East Branch of the DuPage River and then to Swift Road at 7.5 miles out. The off-road trail temporarily ends here, blocked by I-355. A bridge to cross over I-355 is planned. For now though, you have two choices: turn around and head west or take an on-road detour.

For the detour, the DOT recommends heading south .3 mile on Swift Road. Then proceed east on St. Charles Road for 1.1 miles first passing by Churchill Woods Forest Preserve and then crossing both I-355 and Route 53. At West Road, turn left (north) and proceed .4 mile to pick-up the off-road trail again just north of Windsor Avenue in Lombard.

Another alternative is to cross over Swift Road and proceed south by the electric tower into Churchill Woods. There you'll find a mowed turf path through the prairie. Note the sculpted evergreens in the tree nursery to your left. The path leads to a tunnel under St. Charles Road to the forest preserve entrance. From there take St. Charles east as described above.

In Lombard, you'll find 1 mile of off-road trail from West Road to

Grace Street. There the trail temporarily ends. To continue east take another on-road detour south on Grace Street .1 mile to St. Charles Road. Turn left/east on the sidewalk along the Lombard community park for .5 mile to Chase Avenue. The off-road trail resumes on the left (north) side of the road at the intersection of Chase Avenue and St. Charles Place. A narrow dirt path leads to the crushed limestone trail.

The Great Western continues for 1.6 miles to the eastern trailhead at Villa Avenue. The IPP Main Stem and the Villa Park Historical Museum are two blocks south. Total distance from the western to the eastern trailhead (including the on-road detours) is 12.2 miles one-way.

You can cross-country ski on the Great Western Trail in winter; however due to the street crossings, the eastern part is not well-suited for any long distance skiing. When the new multi-use trail through Timber Ridge Forest Preserve is installed in 1995, longer cross-country skiing or hikes will be possible without having to contend with street crossings.

While the Great Western does not compare with the IPP for scenic views for much of its route, it is very well maintained and serves as an effective off-road connecting path with the IPP, the forest preserves, and communities along the way. Call the DuPage County Division of Transportation at 708-682-7318 for more information.

Pratt's Wayne Woods Forest Preserve

More than 3,388 acres of marsh, savanna, woods, and prairie nestled in the far northwestern corner of DuPage County form Pratt's Wayne Woods Forest Preserve. The preserve gets part of its long name from the nearby community of Wayne and from George Pratt who owned much of the land until the mid 1970s. In the late 1920s, the area was excavated for sand and gravel. Later a private fishing and rifle club occupied the property. The forest preserve got its start with a donation of 170 acres by the State of Illinois in 1965.

How to get there:

Take Army Trail Road 1.8 miles west of Route 59. Turn north on Powis Road for .8 mile. The entrance is on the left with parking available near Pickerel Lake.

The preserve supports many interests. Visitors will find a lake and three ponds for fishing, an advanced equestrian jump area, a model airplane field, a dog exercise field, as well as trails for hiking, biking, and cross-country skiing.

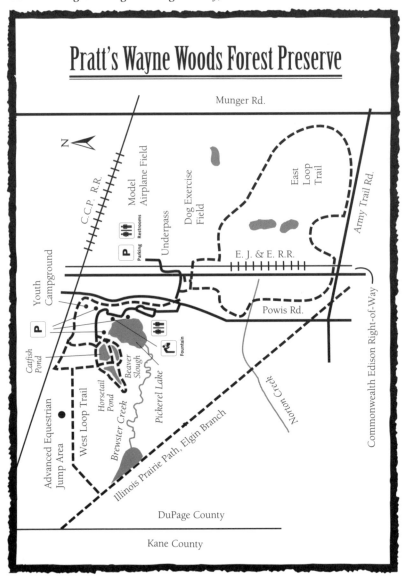

Pratt's Wayne Woods Forest Preserve

A 4.6-mile West Loop Trail can be accessed east of Pickerel Lake and the parking area. Here the path is woodchip surface along and through the woods heading north. After looping around the youth campground area, the trail continues on the service road along

Forest Preserve District of DuPage County

The wetlands at Pratt's Wayne Woods Forest Preserve.

Catfish Pond heading first west, then north then northwest again into the equestrian jump area. The mowed turf trail through the equestrian area is hard to follow and bumpy, but it runs through a very pretty meadow and woodland area. A compass came in handy when I briefly got lost. I would recommend this trail for hiking and mountain bikes only.

After about 1 mile heading west, you'll come to the Elgin Branch of the Illinois Prairie Path (Section 1). Turn left (southeast) to continue on the West Loop Trail which shares the crushed limestone path with the IPP for .9 mile. On your left is a large pond created by Brewster Creek. Here you'll find a scenic view of the wetland areas. On an overcast fall afternoon, I watched a great blue heron fly with slow, labored wing beats low over the marsh, then land next to the water's edge to search for an afternoon snack of fish and frogs. This 4-foot-tall creature with long legs and long neck that curves when it flies is one of the oldest living species of birds on earth. Its cousin, the great white egret, with plumage as bright as snow, also waded along the feeding area as I stopped to watch. Wading birds such as egrets and herons feed in marshes and nest in colonies in secluded wooded islands sometimes as far as several miles away from their foraging grounds. As you continue on the IPP and enter the woods, you might hear the unusual courtship rattle of the sandhill crane in spring and early summer. This state-endangered species quite possibly breeds at Pratt's Wayne Woods. Next, you'll cross over Norton Creek. The West Loop Trail veers off to the left while the IPP continues straight ahead toward the trailhead in Wheaton. The eastern stretch of the loop trail heads north along Powis Road. Since this area is often covered by water, this part of the trail has been closed. Take Powis Road back north to Pickerel Lake from the IPP.

On the east side of Powis Road, near the entrance to the preserve, an asphalt road heads through a tunnel under the E.J.& E. railroad tracks to the special use area. There you will find the model airplane and dog exercise fields as well as the 4.5-mile East Loop Trail. The mowed turf path, frequently used by equestrians, starts on the south side of the service road and runs through prairie and meadow. A road bike won't handle this trail very well. It's better suited for mountain bikes or hiking. Mountain bike enthusiasts should enjoy both loop trails here; but be sure to stay on the 8-foot wide multi-use trails per the forest preserve district rules.

West of the parking area is .6 mile of fishermen trails that wind through woods and around the ponds. These dirt trails are narrow and appropriate for hiking only.

The area around Pickerel Lake is a good place for a picnic with many tables, a shelter, restrooms, and drinking water. The loop trails are open for cross-country skiing in winter.

West Branch, DuPage River Greenway (Mallard Lake, Hawk Hollow, West Branch Forest Preserves and Kline Creek Farm)

Nine forest preserves form an almost continuous river greenway and floodplain in northwestern and west central DuPage County. Wetlands in the floodplains act as natural stormwater retention basins, collecting rain and holding it there as it slowly seeps into the ground. Wetlands also restore the DuPage River's water quality. Plants that thrive in these moist conditions absorb pollutants that would otherwise escape down the river and possibly harm fish and other wildlife. This wetland greenway also provides a scenic, natural area where you can hike, bike, or canoe while viewing nature. From Hanover Park to Naperville, the following DuPage forest preserves surround and protect the river: Mallard Lake, Hawk Hollow, West Branch, Timber Ridge, Winfield Mounds, West DuPage Woods, Blackwell, Warrenville Grove, and McDowell Grove. Other district sites are located farther downstream in Naperville. Together these preserves encompass almost 6,500 acres of open space.

Establishing additional and interconnecting existing trails along the West

Branch of the DuPage River is one of the top priorities of the DuPage County Forest Preserve District. Section 24 describes greenways and some specific plans for additional trails in DuPage County. Someday, hopefully, there will be an 18-mile greenway trail along the river from Mallard Lake near Bloomingdale to the River Walk in Naperville. Several sections are already in place.

West DuPage Woods, Blackwell, and McDowell Grove have extensive trail systems and are described in Sections 6, 8, and 11 respectively. Included in this section are brief descriptions of trails at four preserves. Most are better suited for hiking or mountain bikes. Bicyclists should keep to the 8-foot wide multi-use trails. Mallard Lake, Hawk Hollow, and West Branch have mowed turf or dirt trails around lakes, through meadows, and along the river. Also a new trail is planned at Timber Ridge for completion in 1995.

Mallard Lake Forest Preserve

Nine-hundred and twenty-eight acre Mallard Lake is the first DuPage County forest preserve the river encounters on its journey south.

How to get there:

The entrance is on Lawrence Avenue in Bloomingdale. Take Gary Avenue .8 mile south of Lake Street/Route 20 and north of Schick Road. Head west on Lawrence for .3 mile to the parking area.

Mallard Lake is mostly used for fishing today. Swimming in the 80-acre lake, 7-acre Cloverdale Pond, and the river are bass, catfish, bluegill, crappie, and northern pike waiting to be caught. But you can also hike and bike here. I took a 4-mile walk most of the way around Mallard Lake on my first visit.

There is a short crushed limestone trail near the parking area that leads out to the fishing piers. To the north, you'll find a mowed turf trail which becomes a service road and then a fisherman's trail that loops around most of Mallard Lake. A mountain bike would be more effective given the sometimes rough terrain. There is marshland to the west with cottonwood and huge weeping willow trees along the water.

Drinking water, picnic tables along the lake, and restrooms are available near the parking area. The trail is open for cross-country skiing in the winter.

Hawk Hollow Forest Preserve

Hawk Hollow Forest Preserve in Hanover Park is the next preserve encountered as the river heads west of Mallard Lake.

How to get there:

Take County Farm Road to Schick Road. Head west on Schick Road for .1 mile to Morton Avenue. Turn right (north) on Morton Avenue and proceed .4 mile to the intersection with Lawrence Avenue. Park along Lawrence near the trailhead which is across the street from the community water tower.

Hawk Hollow is a 1,166-acre preserve consisting mostly of open meadows with gently rolling terrain. South of the river are 4.1 miles of mowed turf trails winding through the fields. I didn't see any hawks on my hike, but in late April through mid to late summer you can often see or hear the eastern meadowlark, a common Illinois grassland nester. Listen for a plaintive "see-you-see-see-yer" call and look for a bird with a bright yellow chest sporting a black V. Later on in the summer, the meadowlark may be more difficult to find since it hides its domed nest in a depression in the grasses. To view the meadowlarks and other grassland bird and plant life, you should either hike or use a mountain bike since the trails are somewhat rough in spots. With the watertower looming as a beacon in the distance, you certainly can't get lost.

West Branch Forest Preserve

South of Hawk Hollow near Carol Stream is the 626-acre West Branch Forest Preserve.

How to get there:

Take Army Trail Road to Gerber Road which is east of Route 59 and west of Country Farm Road. The entrance is to the south at the intersection of Army Trail and Gerber.

Deep Quarry Lake is south of the parking area. There is a short crushed limestone trail leading to two fishing piers on the north side of the lake. Beyond that is a dirt trail around the lake which is quite narrow and rocky in spots and, therefore, is not appropriate for even a mountain bike. The hike around the lake is approximately 1.2 miles long. The path along the west bank of the lake runs through a new growth woods and is sandwiched between Deep Quarry Lake and the West Branch of the DuPage River. Bass Lake lies farther west. East of the lakes and river is a .5-mile gravel service road heading south through open fields and slightly rolling terrain. On the west side of the preserve near Klein Road is a 1.3-mile mowed turf trail. Drinking water, picnic tables, and restrooms are available. The multi-use trail is open for cross-country skiing in the winter.

Kline Creek Farm in Timber Ridge Forest Preserve

Following the river south, 1,061-acre Timber Ridge Forest Preserve has both the Elgin Branch of the Illinois Prairie Path and the Great Western Trail passing through it. Also, on the eastern side of the preserve, is Kline Creek Farm.

Forest Preserve District of DuPage County

Bringing home a Christmas tree at Kline Creek Farm.

How to get there:

Take Country Farm Road .5 mile south of St. Charles Road and .6 mile north of Geneva Road. The entrance is west. In 1995, a crushed limestone multi-use trail will be installed in Timber Ridge Forest Preserve from the Illinois Prairie Path near County Farm Road heading north first to Kline Creek Farm and on to the Great Western Trail.

After a short walk from the parking area and crossing over Kline Creek, you'll come to a living example of farm life in the 1890s. Pick up one of the excellent self-guided tour brochures at the information signpost. Hours are Thursday-Monday 9 a.m.–5 p.m. Animal feeding time is at 9 a.m. and 4 p.m. with visitors participating in the afternoon feeding. The chicken coop, barn, large garden, and outdoor privy bring back childhood memories of my grandparents' home in southern Indiana. Visitors can also enjoy a summer kitchen, smokehouse, beekeeping area, pump house, and windmill—all reminiscent of bygone eras. Guided tours of the farm house led by women in period dress normally start hourly at the summer kitchen. Picnic tables, drinking water, and restrooms are available.

West Chicago Prairie Forest Preserve

The DuPage County Forest Preserve District is restoring a 302-acre prairie to look like it did when the Native American hunter encountered it searching for game 200 years ago. Controlled fires and removal of alien plants are helping to return the land to its natural state. It is today one of the finest wet prairies in northern Illinois.

How to get there:

Take Hawthorne Lane west of Route 59 to Industrial Drive. Head south on Industrial Drive for .7 mile. The preserve entrance is on the left. Hikers on the IPP can also access the prairie trails from the Geneva Spur west of Reed Keppler Park in West Chicago. (See Section 1.)

Here, you can walk through several different ecosystems including wet prairie, sedge meadow, marsh, and savanna. Each of these distinct ecosystems provide habitat for unique flora and fauna. The wet grasses are home to the rare prairie white-fringed orchid as well as other flowering prairie plants including the bottle gentian and white lady's slipper. Monarchs and other

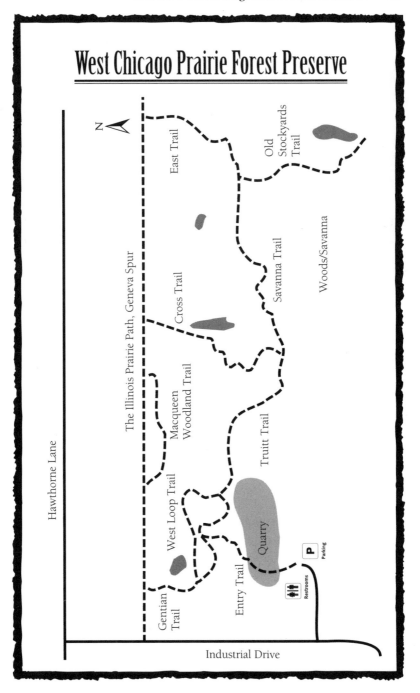

West Chicago Prairie Forest Preserve

N

Hawthorne Lane

The Illinois Prairie Path, Geneva Spur

East Trail

Old Stockyards Trail

Woods/Savanna

Savanna Trail

Cross Trail

Macqueen Woodland Trail

Truitt Trail

West Loop Trail

Quarry

Gentian Trail

Entry Trail

Restrooms

P Parking

Industrial Drive

Forest Preserve District of DuPage County

Shooting stars in bloom in late spring in the West Chicago Prairie.

butterflies sip nectar from wildflowers, adding their orange, black, and yellow colors to the palette of subdued prairie tones. For more information on the flora and fauna of the area, you can find a trail guide published by the forest preserve district at the information signpost.

The trails (2.8 miles) are very narrow and become overgrown in the summer. You may want to wear long pants to avoid scratches. There are no facilities here, so bring a canteen of water if you're hiking on a warm day. The trails are open for hiking and cross-country skiing only.

The West Chicago Prairie Stewardship Group, a volunteer organization, is helping with the restoration and also sponsors birding and field trips through the prairie. Call 708-393-4715 for more information.

West DuPage Woods Forest Preserve

Between Winfield and West Chicago, you'll find trails through a tranquil oak woods and marshland near the West Branch of the DuPage River.

How to get there:

There are two entrances and two separate trails at this 460-acre preserve. One is on the east side of Route 59, one-half mile north of Roosevelt Road/Route 38. The other entrance is farther east. Take Roosevelt Road to Gary's Mill Road. Head northeast .5 mile. The entrance is on the left.

You'll find loop trails at both locations. At the Route 59 entrance, the trailhead is on the north side of the parking lot at a road barricade. The surface is mostly packed earth as the 1.3-mile trail winds its way through a peaceful and shady woods. The path runs along the river through a wetlands area for a short distance. Clearings with picnic tables provide nice spots for a family picnic.

Farther east, starting north of the Gary's Mill Road parking area, the 2.5-mile Elsen's Hill

West DuPage Woods Forest Preserve

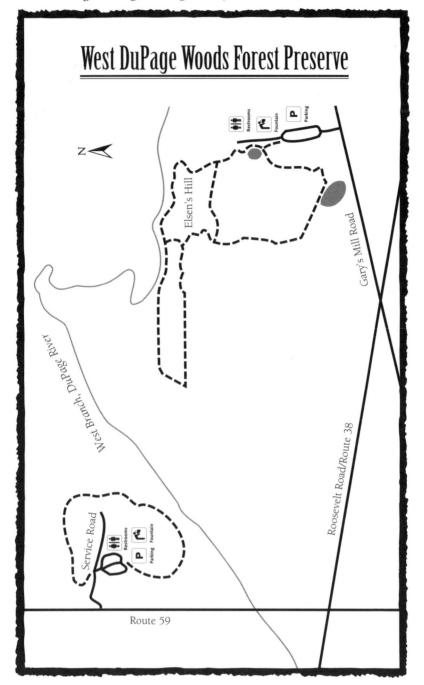

Circle Trail runs through woods and marshes along the river. I saw a lot of deer on the trails here and stumbled upon a startled fawn who exhibited an NBA-quality vertical leap upon my intrusion. The trail surface is partially gravel, mowed turf, and packed earth. If you're on a bike, watch out for the tire ruts near the wetlands. A mountain bike would handle these trails better than my road bike did.

Both areas are quiet and peaceful and were not crowded on my visits. This solitude is welcomed by broad-winged hawks which nest there in summer.

The trails are open for cross-country skiing in the winter. Drinking water and restrooms are available at both trailheads. A new multi-use trail along the river is planned as part of the DuPage River greenway. The Regional Trail in Blackwell Forest Preserve will be extended north through West DuPage Woods to the Winfield Mounds Forest Preserve.

The Wheaton EcoBelt

Wheaton is located in the center of DuPage County. Likewise Volunteer Park, in downtown Wheaton, is the hub and focal point for the IPP. The community park district is developing an EcoBelt, a greenway along Winfield Creek which will run from Community Park in the northeast corner of town through Northside Park, past Cosley Animal Farm, and Lincoln Marsh. A multi-use trail is envisioned that will ultimately serve as a linkage from the Great Western Trail north of Community Park down to the Elgin Branch of the Illinois Prairie Path. While much of this greenway is still in the planning stages, there are existing multi-use trails and bike paths in Wheaton that offer off-road hiking and biking today.

Community Park, north of Geneva Road on President Street, is jointly managed by the Carol Stream, Glen Ellyn, and Wheaton Park Districts. There is a 1.1-mile crushed limestone and mowed turf trail.

Northside Park is west of Main Street just north of the downtown area. Take West Street to the park entrance. Here you'll find a 1.5-mile trail along Winfield Creek. A bridge leads to an island with a log cabin near a 15-acre lagoon. Exercise stations are spread along the trail. A community pool is here as well as a large area of new playground equipment. In the warm weather, the 70-acre park bustles with activity serving as a community gathering spot.

Cosley Animal Farm and Museum is a great place for a walk through 11 acres filled with many domestic farm animals and wild animals in a natural habitat. The wild animals that reside at Cosley have either been injured or raised by humans and as a result are not able to survive in the wild. Also look for an old train depot, an herb garden, an old caboose to explore, and a 130-year-old barn displaying horse drawn vehicles. The entrance is at 1356 Gary Avenue at the intersection with Jewell Road.

Lincoln Marsh Natural Area south of Cosley Farm is 130 acres of natural tranquillity in northwest Wheaton. One and three-tenths miles of woodchip and boardwalk trails wind through the wetlands, woods, savanna, and prairie. Bicycles are not allowed on the nature trail so lock up at the fence rail along the IPP or chain your bike to the railing at the bottom of the boardwalk. More than 300 species of plants and 100 species of animals live in or near the cattail marsh. In spring, you can hear the discordant call of red-winged blackbirds. If sufficient moisture falls in summer, the saw-tooth sunflowers forming a ring around the marsh may grow 10 feet tall or higher.

In the savanna behind the marsh, shooting stars are part of the woodland landscape in spring. Screech and great-horned owls nest in the trees. On a walk at dusk you might hear the low hoot of the great-horned owl. These large hunters of the night begin nesting in winter. Females may lay their eggs in January or February and by April, young owlets may already be in nests begging for a nice meal of field mice.

The Wheaton Park District continues to restore the natural habitat of the marsh and prairie. An environmental center is currently being planned. It will feature an exhibit area, mini-theater, wildlife viewing area, discovery room, laboratory, and classroom where you can understand and better appreciate this unique wetland ecosystem.

The Wheaton EcoBelt

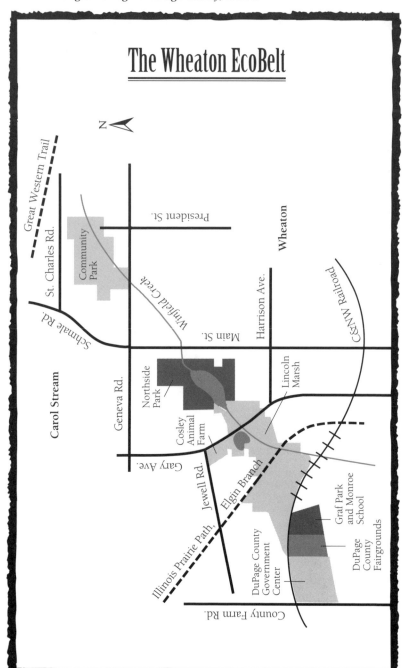

On the trail in the Lincoln Marsh Savanna.

How to get there:

Park near the IPP trailhead at Volunteer Park as described on page 27 in Section 1. The entrance to Lincoln Marsh is on the IPP-Elgin Branch .6 mile northwest of the trailhead at Volunteer Park. Also there is an entrance and parking lot at the intersection of Pierce and Harrison Avenues on the west side of Lincoln Marsh with picnic tables, and a restroom.

For an interesting side trip when hiking or biking the Illinois Prairie Path through downtown Wheaton, head north on Main Street 1 block to the *DuPage County Historical Museum* at the intersection of Main and Wesley Streets. Here you can view a detailed model railroad layout of the major lines crossing DuPage County including the Chicago, Aurora, and Elgin on whose right-of-way the Illinois Prairie Path is based. Three floors of exhibits describe and depict life in DuPage County from the 1830s to the present. Admission is free and a bike rack is available. Call 708-682-7343 for hours and more information.

Another community recreational area, *Atten Park*, can be easily reached from the Aurora Branch of the IPP today. (See page 38 in Section 1.)

Seven Gables Park south of the downtown area has 2.5 miles of asphalt bike path. Located 1.8 miles north of Butterfield Road, the entrance is on the west side of Naperville Road. This is an attractive 70-acre park with exercise stations, shelters, picnic tables, tennis and basketball courts, and baseball fields. The bike path winds through all the activity areas and around a large pond on the southwest side of town.

Two and eight-tenth miles of additional bike paths are planned to interconnect the EcoBelt trails, the community parks, and bike paths. Farther west Graf Park, the DuPage County Fairgrounds, and the DuPage County Center are all on public land that can serve as a route for a multi-use trail connecting with the Aurora Branch of the IPP. Call 708-665-5534 for more information.

The existing trails and bike paths are open for cross-country skiing in the winter. In addition, the Wheaton Park District's 220-acre Arrowhead Golf Course provides approximately 3 miles of set cross-country ski trails which connect to the Herrick Lake and Danada Forest Preserve trails surrounding the golf course. The Arrowhead Golf Course Pro Shop provides ski rentals, lessons and group activities. The Country Tavern restaurant offers shelter, food, and refreshments. Arrowhead Golf Course is located between Herrick Road and Naperville Road on Butterfield Road/Route 56. For more information on Arrowhead, call 708-653-5800. For more information on cross-country skiing in Lincoln Marsh call 708-665-5534.

Blackwell Forest Preserve

While restoring McKee Marsh in 1977, forest preserve employees uncovered the skeleton of a woolly mammoth that roamed the area 14,000 years ago. While you are very unlikely to encounter a woolly mammoth on the trails of 1,311-acre Blackwell Forest Preserve, you may see hawks or eagles soaring above Mt. Hoy, muskrats around the marsh, and myriad other creatures roaming the area.

How to get there:

Take Route 56/Butterfield Road .4 mile west of Winfield Road and east of Route 59. The main entrance is on the north side of the road. On bike, take the Aurora Branch of the IPP. In 1995, a multi-use trail will be installed along Butterfield Road to Blackwell from the IPP Winfield Road crossing. Until then, experienced bicyclists can ride the shoulder on Butterfield Road to the main entrance.

You'll find 7 miles of multi-use trails as well as additional side trails at Blackwell. The Blackwell portion of the Regional Trail (3.3 miles) is 10-foot wide crushed limestone surface. The other paths are mostly mowed turf

Forest Preserve District of DuPage County

McKee Marsh at Blackwell Forest Preserve.

with packed earth sections through the woods as described below.

You can access the Regional Trail west of the parking area near the main entrance. Be careful entering the trail if you're on a bike. There is a sharp dip and curve at the start. Note a large hill, Mt. Hoy beyond the lake, to your right. After passing through a pine grove, you'll come to an abandoned beach area by a large pond. Continuing on, the path leads through a woods with Springbrook Creek on your left. In the spring and early summer, wildflowers proliferate along the creek bank. This is a very peaceful and pretty place. After crossing a bridge over the creek, you'll enter a prairie. A short mowed turf nature trail heads off to the right through the prairie.

After 1.9 miles on the Regional Trail, you'll come to a crossing at Mack Road. Continue straight ahead to McKee Marsh. You may see red-winged blackbirds perched on the cattails and, perhaps, the state-endangered yellow-headed blackbird. This bird, with a golden yellow

Blackwell Forest Preserve

head and two white wing bars, nests in deep marsh areas. The male produces a most unusual, non-lyrical call that sounds like rusty hinges. But to the female, it is a beautiful love song. Listen for the blackbird's loud, raucous call as you walk this 80-acre site which has been significantly restored during the past few years.

Three and two-tenths of a mile out, a grove of majestic oak trees guards the trail. The mowed turf Catbird Trail is an .8-mile loop to the left. A mountain bike or hiking shoes would have been more appropriate than my road bike for this side trail. The path is bumpy from horses and there are some roots on the trail through the woods. The same can be said for the other nature trails in the preserve. Nevertheless it's a quiet, peaceful area running through woods and prairie. (See map on page 69.) The Catbird Trail ends north of McKee Marsh where it intersects both with the Regional Trail which continues on north for another .2-mile and with the 1.4-mile Bob-O-Link Trail that heads east through the prairie and around the marsh. The Regional Trail currently ends at Gary's Mill Road. Plans are to extend the path north to the West DuPage Woods and Winfield Mounds Forest Preserves over the next few years.

Near the northern trailhead of the Regional Trail note the stone monument describing the one room Gary Mills school built in 1851. A pioneer community developed around a grist mill here from 1837 to 1864. In 1994, the Currier School was constructed near where the one-room pioneer school used to stand.

The .5-mile Nighthawk Trail starts east of the school at Gary's Mill Road and heads back south through a tunnel of trees and then rejoins the Bob-O-Link Trail heading first east, then south, then back west as it loops around McKee Marsh. South of the marsh it intersects with the Regional Trail to back track to the parking area near the main entrance.

For a shorter hike through the marsh, there is another parking area north of Mack Road near the canoe launch area. From Butterfield Road, take Route 59 north to Mack Road. Turn right heading east on Mack Road for .2 mile. The McKee Marsh parking area is to your left.

While the McKee Marsh area is native, the Silver Lake/Mt. Hoy section of the preserve offers several manmade attractions. Sixty-acre

Silver Lake, formerly a gravel pit, has developed into a fine place to fish, sail, or canoe. There is a handicapped-accessible asphalt surfaced path along Silver Lake. Nearby Mt. Hoy at 150 feet elevation, is one of the highest spots in DuPage County. While not quite the Rocky Mountains, Mt. Hoy provides a 360-degree scenic view as your reward for a .3 mile hike up the mount on the asphalt trail. No bikes please! Mt. Hoy is well-known as one of the area's best hawk watching spots. In mid-September to early October when winds are from the south, you can often see hundreds of hawks soar overhead from mid-morning to late afternoon. Typically the fourth week of September brings many broad-winged hawks, sometime numbering in the hundreds. These raptors ride the thermals or rising hot air created when weather and topographical conditions are just right. Watching a boiling kettle of broad winged hawks atop Mt. Hoy is witnessing one of nature's most spectacular displays.

As well as being scenic, Mt. Hoy, is also a bit aromatic. The area was used as a landfill for several years. Pipe vents allow the methane gas to escape.

The 1-mile mowed turf Egret Trail is north of Silver Lake near the family camping area. While I didn't see an egret on my visit, a muskrat scurried across the path along Springbrook Creek. The auto road in the preserve, particularly around the camping and picnic area near Winfield Road, is also a good place to bike especially during light use periods.

When the snows come, the trails are excellent for cross-country skiing. When there is a 4-inch base, the forest preserve district opens Mt. Hoy on weekends for snow tubing with the district's rental tubes. Reservable shelters, picnic tables, drinking water, additional parking, and restrooms are available at several locations around Silver Lake and in the family campgrounds. You'll find a pay phone in the campground. There are no drinking fountains in the McKee Marsh area, so bring a canteen on a hot day.

Blackwell is the only preserve or park in DuPage County to provide family camping. The campground is open daily in the summer and on Friday and Saturday nights in spring and early fall. There are 60 campsites, each equipped with a picnic table, fire ring, and gravel parking space. Water, restrooms, and trash containers are nearby. There are no electrical, water, or sewage hookups. With other forest preserves and the IPP nearby, this is a good place for a weekend of hiking and biking. Call 708-790-4900 for more information and at least two weeks in advance for reservations.

Fermilab Bike Path and Nature Trails

Two-hundred years ago, buffalo roamed tall-grass prairie stretching across what is now Du-Page County. Potowatami hunters came south from their villages along the river. Their arrows flew straight and found their mark. This land is presently occupied by the Fermi National Accelerator Laboratory in Batavia. Operated by a consortium of U. S., Canadian, and Japanese Universities, for the U. S. Department of Energy, Fermilab is home to hundreds of scientists from many countries. They focus on high-energy physics—the study of understanding the ultimate building blocks of nature. To help carry out their mission, they built the Tevatron, the "highest energy particle accelerator on earth," then buried it in a 4-mile circumference tunnel. The U. S. Department of Energy acquired cornfields, wetlands, and forest to build the accelerator and required facilities. In 1974, The Nature Conservancy and some local volunteers began reconstructing a tallgrass prairie on 600 acres inside the Tevatron's 4-mile ring. Most of the original prairie had been plowed under by early settlers and farmers to grow corn and other crops. Today 975 acres of tallgrass prairie thrive across the Fermilab site. Additional plantings are anticipated. Controlled burns help maintain the vibrancy of the prairie grasses and wildflowers. You can also wander through or near upland forest, floodplain woods, oak savanna, pasture, croplands, lakes, streams, and wetlands. Because of this diverse habitat, Fermilab harbors 250 species of birds including 80 which breed there regularly. Fermilab is a preferred site for geese, shorebirds, owls, shrikes, and grassland birds.

A 3.6-mile bike path runs through the grounds along Batavia Road. Two prairie trails, .5 mile and 1.2 miles long, lead through part of the reconstructed prairie. The prairie trail connects with 1.8 miles of pathways through a woods to the east.

How to get there:

By auto, take Kirk Road .8 mile north of Butterfield Road to the west entrance or from Route 59 take Batavia Road west to the east entrance. You can also travel to Fermilab on bike or on foot from the IPP. From the Aurora Branch, take the concrete sidewalk/bike path west along Batavia Road starting at the intersection with Butterfield Road in Warrenville 1.9 miles to the east entrance. If you are traveling from the west, take the IPP Batavia Spur to Kirk Road. Head north .8 mile on the asphalt bike path on the west side of Kirk Road. Enter Fermilab at the stoplight at Pine Street.

When you hike or bike through Fermilab, stop at Wilson Hall. You can chain your bike to the railings on either side of the entrance. A giant pendulum, various displays, an information desk, cafeteria, restrooms, and drinking water can be found on the first floor. Take a visitor elevator to the 15th floor to view a video and slide show as well as exhibits about the work done at Fermilab. You will also find an extensive display of arrowheads and other artifacts from the Native Americans that hunted here. Before Fermilab was constructed, August J. Mier, an amateur archaeologist, searched for arrowheads and other Native American implements. He learned by the type of arrowheads found that this land served as a hunting ground for thousands of years. From the panoramic view of the 15th floor windows, you can

Fermilab Bike Path and Nature Trails

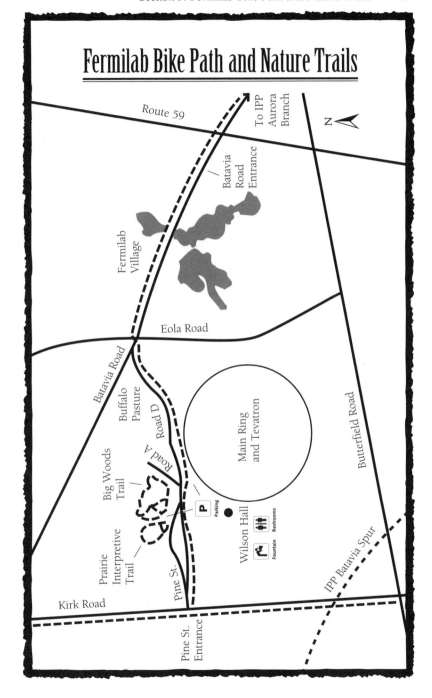

Fermilab Visual Media Services

Herd of buffalo near Wilson Hall.

see the tallgrass prairie, the nature trails and bike path, and the main ring in which the accelerator is housed. On a clear day, the Chicago skyline is visible to the northeast. You can also see something found nowhere else in the Chicago area—a herd of approximately 75 buffalo residing in a pasture northeast of Wilson Hall, a reminder that their ancestors freely wandered here.

The bike path runs 3.6 miles from the east to the west entrance. Along the way, you'll pass two lakes, the Fermilab Village, buffalo grazing in a pasture, Wilson Hall, marsh, woodlands, and the trail-head for the nature trails through the prairie. Most of the bike path is off-road asphalt surfaced, but a section west of Wilson Hall is on-road with a white line separating the bike route from auto traffic.

From Wilson Hall, follow the bike path signs north on Pine Street, a one-way road heading to the west entrance. Here you'll find the prairie trails. In June of 1986, a 50-acre tract was planted with prairie grass seeds. Today Indian grass and big blue stem flourish. A .5-mile wood chipped interpretive trail loops through the prairie. You'll find signs along the way describing the environment and restoration process. Two-hundred species of wildflowers inhabit the prairie. Many of these plants are solely dependent on specific insects which pollinate them. The thousands of insects including butterflies and moths which live here are part of a complex web. In late summer and early fall, you can stand in 7-foot-tall big blue stem and listen to the buzzing sound of insects hidden within the grasses' confines. Big blue stem is nicknamed turkey foot grass because of its stiff turkey foot-like branches.

From the interpretive trail, a 1.2-mile outer loop takes the hiker farther into the prairie. Wandering through this area gave me a sense of what settlers coming to America several centuries ago encountered when they first set foot in this new land.

East of the prairie trail is a 1.8-mile packed earth pathway that loops through a large woods. You can enter the woods from the interpretive trail. The prairie nature trails are open for hiking only. The bike path and forest trails are open for cross-country skiing in the winter.

Call 708-840-3351 for more information.

Herrick Lake and Danada Forest Preserves

Thousands of cars and trucks continuously pass by Butterfield Road and Warrenville Road in a big hurry to get somewhere. One hundred sixty-five years ago these same routes provided trails for the Potowatami to reach their hunting grounds, trading partners, and nearby villages. Today Herrick Lake and Danada Forest Preserves lie between these busy highways and offer an excellent refuge for hiking and biking.

Herrick Lake

Six and one-half miles of crushed limestone trails meander through the woodlands, meadows, wetlands, prairie, and around the lake at this 767-acre preserve. This preserve provides habitat for 300 native plants, 13 fish species, 108 species of birds, as well as 19 mammal species and several different amphibians and reptiles.

How to get there:

By auto, take Butterfield Road to the main entrance just west of Arrowhead Golf Course and .2 mile east of Herrick/Weisbrook Road.

Forest Preserve District of DuPage County

A young cross-country skier at Herrick Lake Forest Preserve.

On bicycle from the Aurora Branch of the IPP at the Weisbrook Road crossing, take the narrow sidewalk on the southwest corner in front of Wheaton-Warrenville South High School. Head south for .5 mile to Butterfield Road. The Regional Trail starts on the southeast corner of Butterfield Road and Herrick/Weisbrook Road entering Herrick Lake.

In 1833, Ira Herrick built his home site amid the tall oaks south of the small settlement of Wheaton. The land was mostly open prairie. Through the years, the prairies were plowed for farming or used for grazing animals.

From 1925 through the 1970s, the land was purchased by the Forest Preserve District. An underground drainage system in the southeast part of the preserve serves to help control flooding and is a marsh home for birds such as the state-endangered black-crowned night heron, frogs, muskrat, and mink.

The Regional Trail runs 2.2 miles through Herrick Lake then continues on through Danada Forest Preserve for another 2 miles east. The Green Heron (1.9 miles), Bluebird (.4 mile), and Meadowlark (1 mile) trails each form loops off the Regional Trail running through the

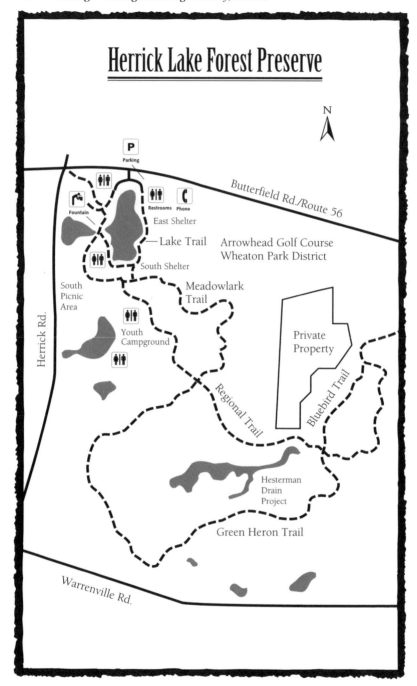

Herrick Lake Forest Preserve

N

Parking

Restrooms Phone

Fountain

East Shelter

Lake Trail

South Shelter

Arrowhead Golf Course
Wheaton Park District

South
Picnic
Area

Meadowlark
Trail

Youth
Campground

Private
Property

Herrick Rd.

Regional Trail

Bluebird Trail

Butterfield Rd./Route 56

Hesterman
Drain
Project

Green Heron Trail

Warrenville Rd.

grasslands and woodlands. A ring-necked pheasant took to flight as I passed nearby on an early fall visit. Fescue grasses here provide nesting habitat for some unusual grassland birds including savanna sparrows and bobolinks, one of Illinois' fastest declining songbirds. Look in late spring and early summer for a black bird with a white stomach and a lemon yellow crown as it flies over the grasses singing its tinkling song to attract a mate.

Farther north is the 1-mile Lake Trail around Herrick Lake. The path runs through the "U" shaped parking lot north of the lake, along the shore, and through some large oak trees near the lake. A very pretty spot!

Drinking water, picnic tables, and restrooms are available at several sites around the lake. A concession stand and boat rental are open throughout the summer on weekdays and from mid-April to mid-October on weekends. Shelters can be reserved and year-round youth camping is also available. The trails are all open for cross-country skiing in the winter.

Danada Forest Preserve

In 1929, the late Daniel and Ada Rice bought 1,350 acres of rolling terrain south of downtown Wheaton. They raised wheat, corn, apples, sheep, cattle, and chickens. But their main focus was thoroughbred racehorses. Today bicyclists, hikers, and cross-country skiers as well as equestrians all enjoy the trails.

How to get there:

By auto, take Butterfield Road to Naperville Road south of Wheaton and north of I-88. The entrance is .6 mile south of Butterfield. Hiking or on a bicycle, take the Regional Trail from Herrick Lake Forest Preserve east to Danada.

As you enter, you will notice that this preserve is unlike most others you may have visited. A 19-room mansion sits to the left. Nearby is a large guard house, barns, stables, and paddocks for the horses. A .5-mile oval training track gave the Rice family thoroughbreds a fine place to hone their skills. Their horses had much success through the years culminating in Lucky Debonair's win in the 1966 Kentucky

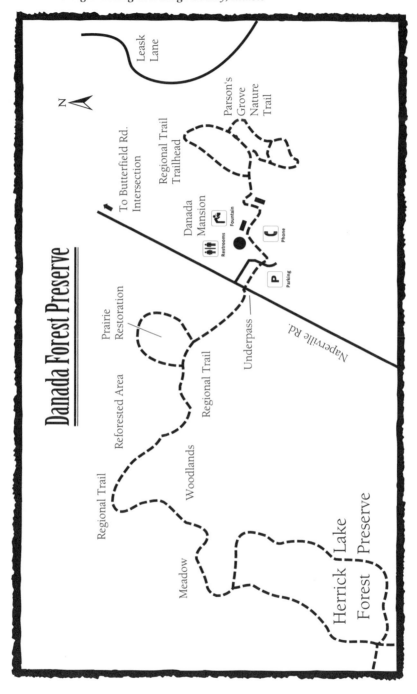

Danada Forest Preserve

Leask Lane

Parson's Grove Nature Trail

To Butterfield Rd. Intersection

Regional Trail Trailhead

Danada Mansion

Fountain

Restrooms

Phone

P Parking

Prairie Restoration

Reforested Area

Regional Trail

Underpass

Napervelle Rd.

Regional Trail

Woodlands

Meadow

Herrick Lake Forest Preserve

Derby. The Danada Equestrian Center, a facility of the Forest Preserve District, has provided programs, training, and a place for DuPage County residents to ride their horses for the last 11 years.

One of my favorite short hikes in the Chicago area is here. Head east on the gravel path by the barn to the right of the mansion. Continue on past a second barn. Head right at the first trail intersection. A .9-mile crushed limestone nature trail winds through the gently rolling terrain of the Parson's Grove area. An oak savanna thrived here before the settlers arrived in the 1830s. The Forest Preserve District is restoring native plants to the area. Beneath the large spreading burr oak trees grow some unusual savanna species including woodland satin grass and golden seal. This area is a delightful, peaceful place to walk.

The eastern trailhead for the Regional Trail is north of Parson's Grove. Plans are to extend the trail farther east to The Morton Arboretum and Hidden Lake Forest Preserve. Today a dirt service road heads east to Leask Lane. Head west from here back through the equestrian center area and take the tunnel under Naperville Road on the westbound Regional Trail. Two miles of multi-use Regional Trail in Danada continue on in Herrick Lake Forest Preserve as described earlier in this section. Be sure you have water before you leave the equestrian center area because the next water fountain is at Herrick Lake 3.2 miles west. After you pass through the tunnel under Naperville Road, you'll see a white fence lining the gravel trail leading to the starting gate for the horse races. Just past the horse track, a .5-mile mowed turf hiking loop trail takes off right (north) through a 35-acre prairie restoration area.

One and four-tenths of a mile west of the tunnel is a Danada trailhead sign. Continue west on the Regional Trail into Herrick Lake Forest Preserve.

Drinking water and restrooms are to the right of the mansion. A pay phone is on the south side of the barn next door. A visitors information signpost is also nearby. The Regional Trail and the Parson's Grove nature trail are open for cross-country skiing in the winter. Seasonal hayrides and sleigh rides are also available. Call 708-790-4900, ext. 202 for reservations and program information.

McDowell Grove Forest Preserve

Fifty years ago, Camp McDowell, northwest of downtown Naperville, was a secret army base for the development and testing of radar. Today you'll find a 422-acre forest preserve there with 5.6 miles of trails through woods and wetlands.

How to get there:

The entrance to McDowell Grove is at the intersection of McDowell Road and Raymond Road 1.1 miles north of Ogden Avenue/Route 34 and south of I-88 and Diehl Road. Entering the preserve, the road crosses a bridge over the West Branch, DuPage River.

A trail through the southern part of the preserve begins east of the parking area (see map). The surface is small gravel at the trailhead with mostly mowed turf in the prairie and packed earth through the woods. The pathway is rough in spots particularly through the prairie with some washout areas. Much of the preserve is in the floodplain. There

McDowell Grove Forest Preserve

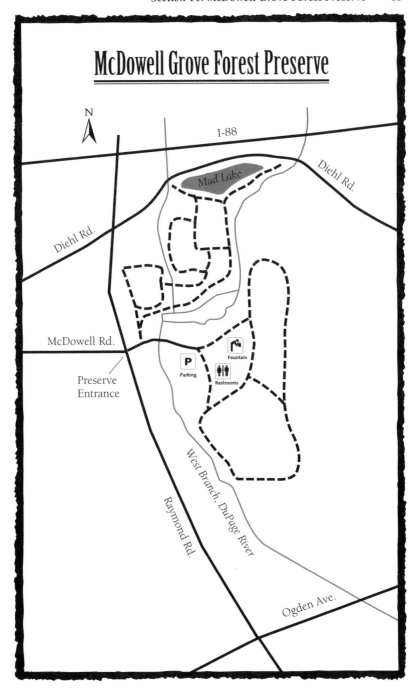

are no trail markers, so a compass will help. But the trail is certainly worth it.

This is a quiet, secluded spot; only occasionally will you pass other trail users. The southwestern portion of the pathway follows a small bluff overlooking the West Branch, DuPage River. Wildflowers and prairie grasses line the trail a good part of the way.

There is also a northern trail that leads to Mud Lake. To access it, bike or hike out to the preserve entrance. The mowed turf trailhead is on the right (north) side of the entrance road. After paralleling Raymond Road through an open field, the trail heads east through the woods on a service road. In winter, look for the Christmas fern, a plant which stays green year-round. Sycamore and butternut hickory trees are also common here. After crossing the river, the pathway heads north to the lake.

A portion of the trail along the lake has recently been improved with a crushed limestone surface. Wildflowers line the water's edge. The trail presently ends at a bridge underpass. Diehl Road and busy I-88 are just north of the lake. In 1995, a 3.7-mile multi-use trail will be installed along the river from Diehl Road at the I-88 underpass south to Ogden Avenue.

There are also narrow and rugged side trails along the river both north and south of the entrance. These paths are not maintained and are not open for biking. Picnic tables, drinking water, restrooms, and reservable shelters are available. The multi-use trails are open for cross-country skiing in the winter.

Naperville Riverwalk, Naper Settlement and Nearby Trails

In March of 1831, Bailey Hobson, his wife Clarissa, and their five children moved from Orange County in southern Indiana to settle near the West Branch, DuPage River in what is now Naperville. Their nearest neighbors were a Potowatami tribe. In July of that year, Joe Naper also settled nearby. By the end of 1832, there were 180 settlers in Naperville, making the community larger than Chicago at the time. Joe Naper laid out the village streets, commanded the local militia, built and operated a saw mill, and served in the Illinois General Assembly. Quite an industrious fellow! No wonder the settlers named their town after him.

Today with the population exceeding 100,000 and growing, Naperville is the largest city in DuPage County. But, with the Naper Settlement Museum Village, the memories of the community's roots and early days are well maintained.

How to get there:

Take the Naperville Road exit south off of I-88 to Ogden Avenue/ Route 34. Head west on Ogden to Washington Street. Go south to Jackson Avenue. Turn right (west) and park in

The Riverwalk along the West Branch, DuPage River in Naperville.

one of the lots along Riverwalk Park. If you are on your bike, there is a large rack next to Centennial Beach one block west on Jackson. Bicycles are not allowed on the Riverwalk pathways.

Along the banks of the West Branch of the DuPage River, the community has built a lovely 2.5-mile brick surfaced Riverwalk. This is a great place to stroll. You'll enjoy fountains, covered bridges crossing the river, flower beds, and the Centennial Beach swimming area. The Riverwalk area is often filled with people enjoying both the natural and man-made beauty of the setting. Information signposts describe the pathways along the river.

The entrance to Naper settlement is two blocks south of the river at the intersection of Webster Street and Porter Avenue. Here you will find "Chicagoland's only living history museum." You can visit reconstructed Fort Payne, built to protect the settlers during the Blackhawk War of 1832 as well as several 19th century homes. An 1841 meeting house has a gallery on the lower level with many paintings that portray the town's evolution from 1831 to 1900. A one-room school house, a brick farmhouse built in 1843, and a replica of an 1830s pioneer log house help the visitor understand what life was like for the early pioneers.

Guides wearing period costumes describe the sites and demonstrate crafts such as blacksmithing and printing as the early settlers performed them. Call 708-420-6010 for hours, admission rates, and other information.

If you're still in the mood for more exercise, you'll find three nearby forest preserves southeast of downtown Naperville that have short trails for hiking.

Pioneer Park

One and six-tenths of a mile south of downtown Naperville on the east side of Washington Street is a small park dedicated to the early settlers. Approximately 1 mile of packed earth trail winds through the woods along the DuPage River. Near the trail, south of the parking area, is a stone monument to Bailey Hobson, the first settler. You'll notice original millstones from the flour mill he built in 1834. Another trail east of the parking area crosses the river and proceeds through the woods for a short distance. You'll find picnic tables and restrooms here, but no water fountain.

Goodrich Woods

Southwest of Pioneer Park is a small, 14-acre forest preserve with a .5-mile trail through a tranquil woods. From Pioneer Park, take Washington Street .2 mile south to Hobson Road. Turn left (east) on Hobson. The Goodrich Woods entrance is .5 mile east of Washington Street on the south side of Hobson.

Egermann Woods

One and seven-tenths of a mile east on Hobson Road from Washington Street is another short trail. The only parking at Egermann Woods is along the highway near the entrance. Don't block the service road if you park there. A mowed turf path runs through a meadow and to the northern border of the preserve.

There are no facilities at either Goodrich Woods or Egermann Woods but both are quiet, secluded spots for a walk through the forest.

Greene Valley Forest Preserve

South of Lisle and west of Woodbridge lies the 1,425-acre Greene Valley Forest Preserve. Almost 7 miles of multi-use trails are open for hiking and biking.

How to get there:

Take 75th Street west of Route 53 and turn south on Greene Road. Turn right (west) on 79th Street. Turn left (south) on Thunderbird Road which leads to the parking area at the trailhead.

Daniel Greene and his wife settled on 250 acres here in 1835. A nephew's farmhouse built in 1853 still stands at the far northern section of the preserve at the intersection of Greene and Hobson Roads. In the wooded area north of 79th Street, you'll find an oak forest. Wildflowers proliferate in the spring.

The trails are mostly mowed turf. A map will be helpful since several trails intersect along the way. The pathways lead mostly through open prairie, savanna, and marsh with a stretch along the East Branch, DuPage River. Anderson Creek

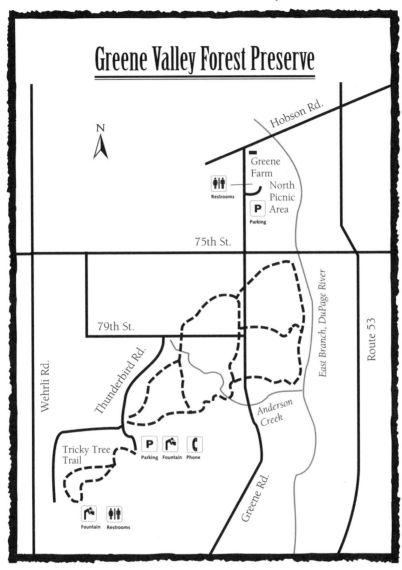

Greene Valley Forest Preserve

runs through the preserve and empties into the river near the trail. Fox, coyote, and many other wildlife have been discovered in the preserve.

There is also a short self-guided nature path—Tricky Tree Key Trail—located in the Thunderbird Youth Camp in the southwestern

Forest Preserve District of DuPage County

Greene Valley Forest Preserve

portion of the preserve. Starting from the south parking area in the campground, interpretive signposts will test your tree knowledge and display sayings about woods and trees from famous philosophers, humorists, naturalists, and young students. An example, " 'You will find something more in the woods than in books. Trees will teach you that which you can never learn from masters. I have no other masters than the maples and the oaks.' St. Bernard of Clairvaux." The 1-mile trail through the heavily wooded youth camp area is open to hikers only. Drinking water, restrooms, a public phone, and a guard residence are located in the youth camp area. Please respect the privacy of the campers.

A picnic area is available in the northern portion of the preserve. Take Greene Road north of 75th Street. The entrance is to the right. The trails are open for cross-country skiing in the winter. A 2.4-mile crushed limestone surfaced trail is planned for construction along the river from Hobson Road to the Will County border by the end of 1996.

The Morton Arboretum

F ANTASTIC! If you enjoy hiking in the woods and want to learn more about trees, this is the place for you.

How to get there:

The Arboretum is located north of I-88 and west of I-355 in Lisle. Both highways are clearly marked with directional signs to the Arboretum entrance on Route 53.

The story of The Morton Arboretum actually starts in Nebraska in the late 19th century. J. Sterling Morton, a pioneer newspaper man who later became acting governor and U. S. Secretary of Agriculture under President Grover Cleveland, encouraged local Nebraska farmers to plant trees. Arbor Day evolved out of his promotional efforts. His sons, particularly, Joy Morton, inherited their father's love of trees. After moving to Chicago and making his fortune by founding and managing the Morton Salt Company, Joy built a country estate, Thornhill

The Morton Arboretum Logo

Farm, in DuPage County. He envisioned gathering together in one location all trees and shrubs from throughout the world that would grow in the northeastern Illinois climate. In the first year of development, 138,000 trees were planted. Today there are more than 3,000 varieties of trees and shrubs spread over 1,500 acres of gently rolling hills.

A visitor could easily spend a week and only begin to really appreciate all that this special place has to offer. A one-way road meanders through the Arboretum for 12 miles with 27 stops at parking areas along the way. This provides easy access to many different trails, woody plant collections, a prairie, and to Thornhill in the northwestern section. Here a portion of the old Morton mansion remains as a Founders Room with displays and information about the Morton family. Spread throughout the Arboretum are 25 miles of hiking trails ranging from a short walk through the Fragrance Garden at Thornhill to a hike of 2.9 miles on the three loops of the Illinois Trees Nature Trail.

You will receive a map and visitors guide as you enter. More detailed maps and guides can be purchased at the Visitor Center for a nominal fee. A theater with free half-hourly slide shows that last 10-20 minutes and change with the seasons is adjacent. This is a good stop for first-time visitors.

We've included a brief summary of the major trails.

- Illinois Trees Trail – Northeast of the Visitor Center are three loop trails celebrating our native trees. Large wooden signposts displaying trail maps are at all major trail intersections. This walk is particularly lovely in early to mid-October when maples turn golden yellow to bright red.

  Loop #1 (.6 mile) – Starts at the Visitor Center and loops around Meadow Lake on an asphalt pathway. You'll encounter specimens of many local trees with information displays and benches along the way. This is a great way to learn more about trees indigenous to northeastern Illinois including tulip, redbud, red maple, and wild black cherry.

William Stickney, Courtesy The Morton Arboretum

Illinois Tree Trail at The Morton Arboretum.

Loop #2 (1 mile) – Woodchip trail with some very moderate climbs. Spring flowering shrubs and wildflowers are along the pathway.

Loop #3 (1.2 mile) – Somewhat more strenuous through a beautiful oak-maple forest. You'll pass near Bur Reed Marsh. This woods has excellent fall colors. Woodchip surface.

• Geographic Trail (.9 mile) – The trail, which can be hard to follow with a mowed turf surface, leads to collections of woody plants from Appalachia, the Balkans, Asia, and eastern U. S. wetlands.

• Big Rock Trail (.9 mile) – The woodchip trail meanders through an oak forest to a huge boulder that was carried here from Canada during the last glacial period. Along the way, my wife and I saw the largest mushroom we've ever encountered. About 16 inches long, 1 foot wide, and shaped like a white football helmet, a huge puff ball pushed its way through the forest floor laden with fallen leaves.

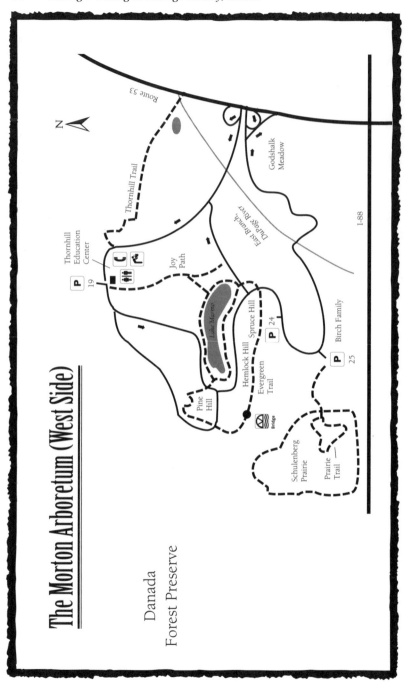

The Morton Arboretum (West Side)

Danada Forest Preserve

Route 53

N

Thornhill Trail

Thornhill Education Center

P 19

Joy Path

East Branch DuPage River

Godshalk Meadow

I-88

Lake Marmo

Pine Hill

Hemlock Hill

Spruce Hill

P 24

Birch Family

P 25

Evergreen Trail

Bridge

Schulenberg Prairie

Prairie Trail

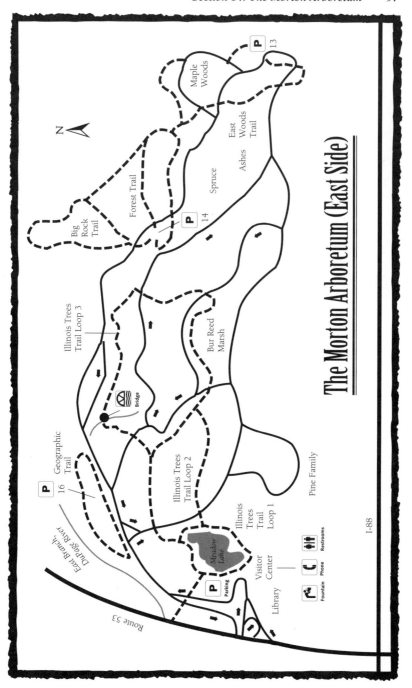

The Morton Arboretum (East Side)

John Kohout, Courtesy The Morton Arboretum

Oak Savanna on Arboretum's West Side.

- Forest Trail (.7 mile) – A woodchip loop trail through the woods. All three trails on the northeast side (Big Rock, Forest, and East Woods) are connected by side trails.

- East Woods Trail (1.1 mile) – The path runs through a sugar maple woods with lovely fall colors. Take a map and compass because it's easy to get on a side path leading to the Forest Trail. But you can't get seriously lost since the auto road cuts through the forest areas.

- Prairie Trail (.7 mile) – The Schulenburg Prairie is beautiful. A brochure is available at the Visitor Center to describe what you'll see at markers along the way. Arboretum naturalists restored the prairie and nearby oak savanna. The result is a collage of wildflowers, prairie grasses, butterflies, bumble bees, and dragonflies. Small concrete grids have been placed on the main trail to help keep your feet dry and the trail from being overgrown in the summer. Side trails run through and around the prairie's perimeter.

- Evergreen Trail (.9 mile) – A woodchip-surfaced trail along Lake Marmo with a small waterfall leads through forests of spruce, pine, and hemlock. There is a fairly steep climb to the Pine Hill area. Bird watchers annually scout the evergreens here for a small winter visitor, the northern saw-whet owl.

- Ozark Area Trail (.5 mile) – Mowed turf and woodchip trail along Lake Jopamaca with flowering dogwoods in the spring.

Shorter Walks
- Horticulture Display Gardens – South of the Visitor Center are ground cover, hedge, woody herb, and other gardens.

- Thornhill Area – Take the brick walk through the Fragrance Garden or the crushed limestone Joy Path to see perennial gardens.

After a strenuous hike, enjoy lunch at the Ginkgo Restaurant and Coffee Shop in the Visitor Center. Nearby is the Sterling Morton Library open to the public Monday through Saturday. Classes, special events, and programs are offered year-round. Call 708-719-2400 for more information. There is a parking fee, but it's certainly worth it.

A picnic area, drinking fountains, restrooms, and public telephone are available. The trails are not open for bicycling or cross-country skiing.

Downer's Grove Area Preserves
(Lyman Woods and Maple Grove)

Maple Grove Forest Preserve

You can see a maple forest that survived amid oak savannas and open prairie while taking a pleasant walk through the woods at Maple Grove Forest Preserve.

How to get there:

Take 56th Street/Maple Avenue .7 mile west of Main Street in Downers Grove and east of I-355. The entrance is on the north side of Maple Avenue.

Signs along the packed earth trail starting on the east side of the picnic area describe how a prairie slowly evolves to woodlands. First elm and ash flourish. These trees require much sunlight to shine through for the young saplings to take hold. As the forest matures, red and white oak dominate. Finally sugar maple and basswood prevail. These species need little sunlight to filter through to the forest floor. Typically one finds only oak groves in a native prairie or savanna area. The burr oak has a thick fire-resistant bark that enabled it to survive the frequent prairie fires.

North of the parking area next to the information signpost is the start of a crushed limestone path heading north. At a "y" intersection, the trail

Forest Preserve District of DuPage County

Maple Grove Forest Preserve.

splits into east and west directions. Heading east will lead to the interpretive trail mentioned above. The path west leads to a bridge over a creek and ends near the Gilbert Park playground area. As well as learning a bit of botany, you'll have a relaxing 1-mile hike through the forest. Side trails can extend your visit to the woods.

This is one of the few sugar maple woods in DuPage County and one of the best places to view fall colors. Sugar maple leaves turn yellow and red in autumn when chlorophyll, the green pigment involved in the tree's food-making process, stops getting produced. Then the autumn hues, which are masked by the more dominant green in summer, can shine through. On a bright mid-October day you can walk through the maple woods as it rains gold all around you. Given its location and woods, this preserve is a popular picnic spot. Drinking water, picnic tables, and restrooms are available.

Lyman Woods Natural Area

Take a hike through Lyman Woods in late May and early June and you'll see many spring wildflowers including trillium. These spring

Lyman Woods Natural Area

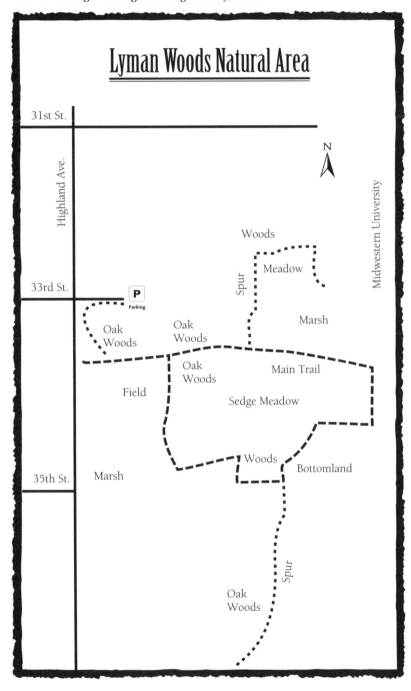

flowers pop up in the woods before trees leaf out and hide the sun from the forest floor.

How to get there:

The parking area is .6 mile south of Butterfield Road/Route 56 and north of Ogden/Route 34 on Highland Avenue. The entrance is on the east side of Highland at 33rd Street in Downers Grove.

The Downers Grove Park District manages this 90-acre site in cooperation with the Forest Preserve District of DuPage County and the Village of Downers Grove. The involved agencies are restoring prairie, marsh, and savanna. You will find .8 mile of main trail and .5 mile of spur trails through oak forest, meadow, and marsh. The trail surface is mostly packed earth and mowed turf. At an information signpost, you can pick up a trail guide displaying the wildflowers you will see in spring and summer. Two long boardwalks take the hiker over a marsh area. On the main trail, you'll come out of the woods to an interesting spot. A duckweed-surfaced pond in the marsh with dead tree trunks protruding from the green morass cast a surreal setting.

A compass is helpful since there are several trail intersections. Follow the trail markers along the main trail. The two spur trails are one-way so a bit of back tracking is required through the oak woods and the meadow (see map). The eastern portion of the main trail briefly runs along a field at the border of Midwestern University's campus.

There are no facilities here so bring a canteen. The trail is open to hikers only. Many nature programs are offered throughout the year at Lyman Woods by the Downers Grove Park District. Call 708-963-1300 for more information.

Willowbrook Wildlife Center

Willowbrook Wildlife Center, a facility of the Forest Preserve District of DuPage County, is a home and rehabilitation center for injured animals. Visitors can closely view some 30 species of native animals of DuPage County including great-horned owl, barred owl, and red fox. Rehabilitators release animals back into the wild once their health is restored.

How to get there:

Willowbrook Wildlife Center is in Glen Ellyn .6 mile west of Route 53. Take Park Boulevard either south from Roosevelt Road/Route 38 or north from Butterfield Road/ Route 56. The entrance is on the east side of Park at the 22nd Street intersection.

Kids of all ages will enjoy the indoor animal exhibits. My eight-year-old son would have stayed here all day! We saw a green-backed heron eating fish. We learned that blue jays help oak trees proliferate by carrying acorns in their mouths for long distances. We visited the

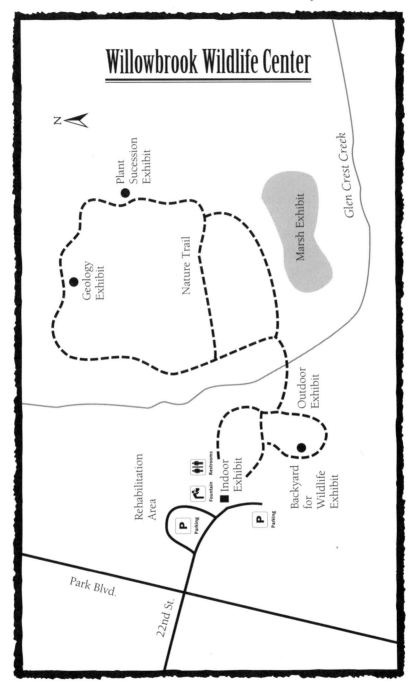

Willowbrook Wildlife Center

Jeff visiting the animals at Willowbrook Wildlife Center.

Possum Hollow room with animal displays, books, and molds of animal tracks. There is also a microscope to view butterflies, insects, and small animal skeletons. Outside we saw a golden eagle that could no longer fly, woodchucks, a barred owl, and a great-horned owl.

North of the outdoor animal exhibit area is a bridge over Glen Crest Creek to a .6-mile crushed limestone nature trail. Check out the geology, plant succession, and marsh exhibits as well as the prairie restoration project. At the geology exhibit, we saw granite stones that were carried here from as far north as Ontario, Canada by the great glacier 20,000 years ago. Laminated trail guides and animal descriptions provide more information. On one summer walk, we found a small fox snake stretched out across the crushed limestone trail. Nudged by a small stick thrown in its direction, the snake slithered into the meadow. Later we saw an adult fox snake in one of the indoor exhibits.

Nature programs are available year-round. Willowbrook is open from 9 a.m.-5 p.m. daily except for Thanksgiving, Christmas Eve, Christmas Day, and New Year's Day. Water, picnic tables, public phone, a bike rack, and restrooms are available.

Churchill Woods Forest Preserve

At Churchill Woods you can walk through a white oak forest along the East Branch, DuPage River. Here a tribe of several hundred Potawatami lived in a village near the river until 1835.

How to get there:

Take I-355 to North Avenue. Travel east for .3 mile to Route 53. Head south on Route 53 for 1.5 miles to St. Charles Road. Turn right (west) on St. Charles. After crossing over I-355, you'll find parking areas on the left (south) along St. Charles Road.

Deacon Winslow Churchill, his wife Mercy, along with their sons, daughters, and grandchildren moved from New York to the Babcock Grove area just north of the Potawatami village in 1834. They bought a large parcel of land for $1.25 per acre. The Churchill family farmed the land for more than 100 years through several generations. In 1936, a portion of the property was acquired by the Forest Preserve District.

One of only a few native prairies left in DuPage County occupies the northern portion of this 260-acre preserve. The southern part is a mixture of woods and wetlands with more than

Churchill Woods Forest Preserve

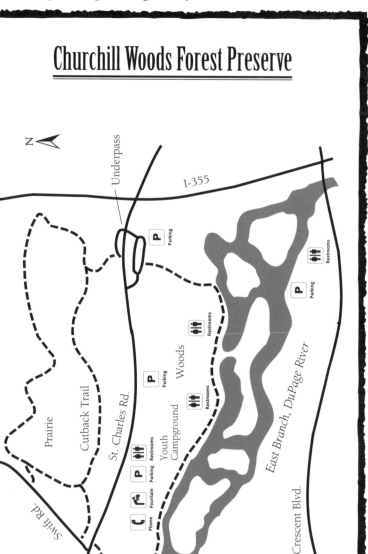

2 miles of river frontage.

The 2-mile main trail is a loop through woods, along the river, and through the prairie. The trail surface is a combination of crushed limestone, mowed turf, woodchip and packed earth. A good place to start is at the parking area closest to I-355. The trail is open to hikers and cyclists. You may want to do both—on your bike to get the layout and repeat on foot to better observe the wildflowers and waterfowl along the way. Head south from the parking lot on the crushed limestone trail through the woods. Dutchman's breeches grow in early spring, while yellow touch-me-nots or pale jewelweed proliferate in late summer, offering nectar to hummingbirds and other wildlife. After blooming, the jewelweed produces long-seeded pods that spring open when touched. At the shelter house, the main trail continues to the right (west) along the river. A short side trail to the left (east) starts at the end of the grassy area and heads south along the river to Crescent Boulevard at the southeast corner of the pre-serve. You'll need to back track to the main trail at the shelter house.

From the shelter, the main trail continues west along the river through the picnic areas for about .5 mile to the campground. The "trail" through the picnic area is basically mowed turf along the river. Here the traffic sounds from I-355 subside and woodland bird songs start to dominate. Past the camp area, a packed earth pathway enters a new-growth woods and then turns north. Stay on the main path to the right. There is a street crossing at St. Charles Road near the inter-section with Swift Road. The main trail picks up again about 20 feet north on the east side of Swift Road and heads east through wood-lands 500 feet to a trail intersection.

The path to the left leads through the second largest native prairie in the county—next to the West Chicago Prairie Forest Preserve site. In spring and summer, you'll find many wildflowers growing throughout the 34 acres of this designated state nature preserve. If you bend close to the grasses, you might inhale the fragrance of wild mint in summer. Or look for a stand of bottle gentian. This late-blooming wet prairie wildflower displays a purple shade that con-trasts the more subtly-colored grasses. Back at the previously men-tioned intersection, if you head right (east), you will come to a

Forest Preserve District of DuPage County

East Branch, DuPage River at Churchill Woods Forest Preserve.

cutback trail leading into the woods where the sun filters through the trees onto a dark pathway.

After completing the cutback and the mowed turf path through the prairie, proceed south on the main trail at the east end of the preserve past the Forest Preserve District's Northeast Sector Ranger Center. Head to your left on the asphalt service road to take a tunnel under St. Charles Road back to the parking area. As in all other forest preserves, this trail is not designed for racing. Bicyclists please use caution and travel slowly at intersections and curves. If you are visiting with young children, you may want to forgo the street crossing on St. Charles by using the tunnel both going to and returning from the prairie.

Picnic tables, restrooms, and drinking water are available. Also there is a public telephone at the campground parking area farthest to the west. The trails are open for cross-country skiing in the winter.

Meacham Grove and Spring Creek Reservoir Forest Preserves

In north central DuPage County, near Roselle and Bloomingdale, are two DuPage Forest Preserves with 1-mile trails.

Spring Creek Reservoir

This is a good place to bring youngsters just starting out on a bike or for anyone on a short hike.

How to get there:

Take Lake Street/Route 20 one mile west of I-355 and .2 mile east of Glen Ellyn Road. The entrance is on the north side of the highway across from Glendale Country Club.

A 38-acre lake serves as a flood control site for Springbrook Creek which flows into the reservoir via a huge spill-way. Approximately 40 feet above the lake's surface is a 1.2-mile asphalt path that loops around the reservoir. Tall trees border the preserve on three sides. In the summer, a yellow and pink carpet of clover and goldenrod fills the banks leading down to the water. The trail is also popular for in-line skating. Benches along the path, drinking water, picnic tables, a shelter, and restrooms are available.

Meacham Grove

West of Spring Creek Reservoir is a 231-acre woods featuring a peaceful 1-mile trail. In fall, you can enjoy the changing colors of the sugar maples. In spring, a host of wildflowers such as red and great white trillium blanket the forest floor while colorful migrating warblers search the tree tops for insects to sustain them on their way north to nesting grounds.

How to get there:

The entrance is on the west side of Bloomingdale Road south of Irving Park Road and .4 mile north of Lake Street in Bloomingdale.

The forest preserve information signpost identifies a .6-mile trail but you can extend it to 1 mile or more with side paths and a service road. Follow the arrows on the trail markers along the packed earth and gravel pathway through the woods. A service road heads west to Rosedale Road. Drinking water, picnic tables, and restrooms are available.

When the snows come, you can cross-country ski at both locations.

Northeastern Forest Preserve Trails

Salt Creek runs south through eastern DuPage County. Restoration of the stream as a natural greenway is one of the top priorities described in the Northeastern Illinois Regional Greenways Plan (Section 24). A trail system along Salt Creek north to Ned Brown Forest Preserve in Cook County and southeast past Brookfield Zoo to the Des Plaines River is envisioned. Today three forest preserves in northeastern DuPage County have trails along or near Salt Creek.

Salt Creek Park

West of Wood Dale, there is a 1.7-mile trail through the Salt Creek bottomlands.

How to get there:

Take Villa Avenue or Addison Road to Elizabeth Street north of the Maple Meadows Golf Course. The preserve entrance is on the north side of Elizabeth .2 mile east of Addison Road.

As you enter in early spring, inhale the fragrance emanating from the blooming wild hyacinths. Mowed turf/packed earth trails head east from the parking area into the woods. Also a gravel trail heads west to Addison Road with a bridge crossing over Salt Creek. Two predators, the red-tailed hawk and the great-horned owl, nest in these mature woods. Because of some special adaptations, they coexist peacefully. First, red-tailed hawks hunt during the day while the owls search for food at night, so neither species encroaches on the other's hunting grounds. Secondly, red-tailed hawks build their nests in spring, then leave in summer after the young have fledged. In late fall and early winter, a great-horned owl pair may move into the hawk's ready-made nest. By April, the young owls are ready to leave the nest and the hawks can return to begin raising a new family.

A water fountain, picnic tables, two shelters, and restrooms are available.

Wood Dale Grove

South of the community of Wood Dale is a 160-acre preserve with a trail around a lake and through woods.

How to get there:

Take Wood Dale Road .3 mile south of 3rd Avenue. The entrance is on the east side of Wood Dale Road north of Lake Street.

A 1.2-mile trail loops around the 7-acre lake and through a forest. A crushed limestone surface was recently added. Benches along the way are good spots to relax. In one location, the bench by the trail overlooks a tallgrass prairie where forbs (prairie flowers) bloom spring through fall. On a mid-October hike, the lake was filled with several hundred Canada geese. Their honking does not quite drown out the sound of jets overhead reminding us that O'Hare International Airport is just a few miles away.

Cricket Creek
How to get there:

Take Route 83 south of I-290 to North Avenue. Head west on North Avenue to Villa Avenue. Proceed north (right) on Villa to Fullerton Avenue. Make a right turn on Fullerton. After crossing over a bridge, the parking area is on the north side. From the west take Route 53 to Fullerton and head east past Villa Avenue to the entrance.

A newly installed 1.4-mile crushed limestone trail runs south along the east bank of Salt Creek starting at Fullerton and ending near North Avenue. The path encircles three retention ponds that must be filled with fish given the number of people fishing there. Eventually the trail will be extended south to connect with the IPP in Villa Park just east of Route 83. Also there is a short asphalt path north of the parking area on Fullerton Avenue. Playground equipment, picnic tables, a shelter, a water fountain, and restrooms are available near the entrance.

All three preserves are open for cross-country skiing.

Salt Creek Greenway Trail and York Woods Forest Preserve

Two trails along or near Salt Creek can be found in Elmhurst and at a nearby DuPage Forest Preserve north of Oak Brook.

Salt Creek Greenway Trail

In 1992, the Elmhurst Park District installed a woodchip hiking trail along Salt Creek.

How to get there:

Take Butterfield Road .3 mile east of Route 83. Turn left (north) on Spring Road. You'll find a parking area on the west side of Spring in Eldridge Park.

One mile of asphalt pathway loops around Eldridge Park's ball fields, tennis courts, up a sledding hill, and along Salt Creek. In the northwestern section of the park, a woodchip trail heads north along the east bank of Salt Creek. The trail runs 1.1 miles along the creek through woods and near residential areas to Sleepy Hol-

low Park where the off-road trail ends. Follow Rex Boulevard .3 mile north to the Illinois Prairie Path-Main Stem Branch (Section 1).

Drinking water and restrooms are available in Eldridge Park. The trail is open for cross-country skiing in the winter.

York Woods Forest Preserve

The oldest preserve in DuPage County, York Woods, was acquired in 1917. Surrounded by I-88 as well as Routes 38, 56, and 83, this 61-acre woodland on the north side of Oak Brook manages to retain its tranquillity as the cars and trucks go racing by.

How to get there:

East of Route 83 and Route 56, take the York Road exit south off Roosevelt Road/Route 38. The south area entrance is left on Harger Road, the first exit off York Road.

Carl Sandburg, noted poet and biographer, wrote some of his work here many years ago while living in an old home on the property. Now there is a 1.2-mile asphalt loop trail connecting two picnic areas. The pathway runs through a shady oak woods and mown grass fields in the picnic areas. This is a good place for a short hike with youngsters.

Drinking water, picnic tables, and restrooms are available in both picnic areas. The trail is open for cross-country skiing in the winter.

An Oak Brook bike path starts on Harger Road south of the forest preserve and runs west to the Oak Brook Center. (See Section 21.)

Oak Brook Bike Path

Oak Brook is well known for its lovely outdoor shopping mall, Butler National Golf Course, McDonald's Hamburger University, and attractive residential neighborhoods. The community also has an excellent pedestrian/bike path system.

How to get there:

Bike path routes are spread throughout Oak Brook. A good place to park is at the park district central location west of Butler National. Take 31st Street/Oak Brook Road east of Route 83. Turn left (north) on Jorie Boulevard. Turn left again at the next street which is Forest Gate Road. A parking area is to your right. The Oak Brook pedestrian/bike path system consists of 10 miles of off-road path and 5 miles of designated on-road bike route. Here we describe the pathway around the Butler International Sports Core and through the park district area to the west as well as bike routes leading to two forest preserves.

You can access the bike path on the east side of Jorie Boulevard near the parking area. Take the asphalt

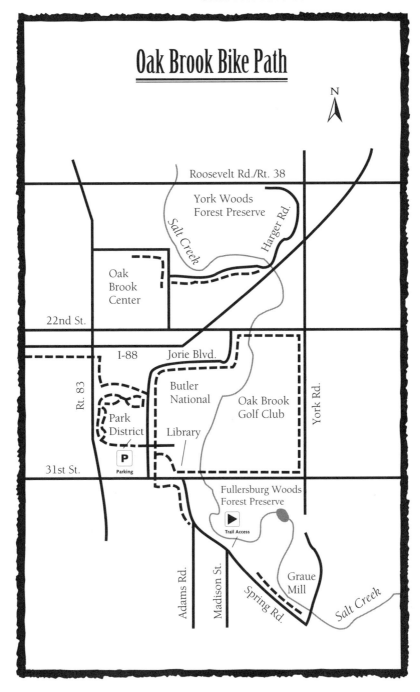

Oak Brook Bike Path

path north by the entrance to McDonald's Hamburger University. Just beyond the entrance is a pretty view of a lake on the campus. Follow the pathway first west and then back north to 22nd Street and then east along 22nd Street. You will first past Butler National Golf Course and then the Oak Brook Golf Club. Evergreens, mostly spruce and some pine, line the trail and, hopefully, block the errant golf ball from landing on a trail user. Along the way, you will cross over Salt Creek as it meanders south through the golf course. The path surface is a well-maintained mixture of asphalt and crushed limestone around the Sports Core. At the intersection of 22nd Street and York Road, follow the path running south between York Road and the Oak Brook Golf Club. At the intersection of York Road and 31st Street, head right (west) along 31st Street. The forest across the street is part of Fullersburg Woods Forest Preserve. The bike path crosses over Salt Creek again and then runs behind the community library at the Spring Road intersection. Continuing straight ahead will take you back to Jorie Boulevard just south of the parking area. The loop around the Sports Core is a 4.6-mile trip.

At the intersection of Spring Road and 31st Street, the bike path heads south on the west side of Spring Road leading to Fullersburg Woods Forest Preserve. The first .3 mile south of 31st Street is an off-road crushed limestone surface trail to the Adams Road intersection. Continue southwest on Spring Road for another .3 mile to the Madison Street intersection. On your left is a trail entrance into Fullersburg Woods (Section 22).

Another portion of the bike path farther north leads from York Woods Forest Preserve southwest to the Oak Brook Center. From the York Woods south area entrance (see Section 20), head south on Harger Road. After crossing Salt Creek, the dedicated bike path along the east side of Harger leads to Spring Road and the Oak Brook Center.

Another good place to bike or hike is in Central Park in the Oak Brook Park District area west of Jorie Boulevard. The asphalt path heading west from the parking area extends to Route 83 and then loops south and then back east. Along the way, you'll encounter several ponds formed by Ginger Creek. The bike path runs around the ponds which are often monopolized by Canada geese.

Spread throughout the bike path are several tunnels which offer safe passage under the busy roadways. The pathways are well marked with signs along the way. The off-road sections are open for cross-country skiing in the winter.

The map on page 119 shows only the portion of the bike path described here. Call the Oak Brook Park District office at 708-990-4233 for more information or to get a map which shows several additional miles of bike path.

Fullersburg Woods Forest Preserve and Graue Mill

Located between the communities of Oak Brook and Hinsdale is an oasis of natural beauty, Fullersburg Woods. Spend a day hiking, biking, and visiting Graue Mill, Illinois' only operating waterwheel grist mill, and the Environmental Education Center.

How to get there:

You'll find two places to park. The Graue Mill entrance is south of 31st Street on York Road just north of Odgen Avenue. The Fullersburg Woods entrance is on Spring Road also south of 31st Street and north of Ogden Avenue. If you are bicycling or hiking on the Oak Brook bike path, take the Spring Road route south to the forest preserve trail system (see Section 21).

Salt Creek meanders through the woods of this 221-acre nature preserve. You'll find 5 miles of trails here. Starting from the Graue Mill parking area, the 2.5-mile multi-use trail heads northwest along the west bank of the

Forest Preserve District of DuPage County

Graue Mill at Fullersburg Woods Forest Preserve.

creek. A tunnel under Spring Road leads to the mill. On the other side of the parking lot near the restrooms is the Ben Fuller house, built around 1840. One of the oldest homes in DuPage County, the building is being restored to serve as a museum.

Graue Mill is a working grist mill built by Herbert Graue from 1848 to 1852. The Graue family operated the mill through three generations until 1912. You'll discover artisans in period costume spinning and weaving and producing stone-ground cornmeal. Graue Mill and Museum, a national historic landmark, is owned by the Forest Preserve District of DuPage County and operated by the Du-Page Graue Mill Corporation. Hours are 10 a.m. to 4:30 p.m. daily from mid-April to mid-November. Call 708-655-2090 for more information about programs, field trips, and admission fees.

The multi-use trail heads northwest from Graue Mill through the woods and along the creek bank. There are hills. Some are fairly steep. In one section the trail climbs a bluff overlooking Salt Creek. Short spurs from the main trail run out to Spring Road on the western side of the preserve and to 31st Street on the north side.

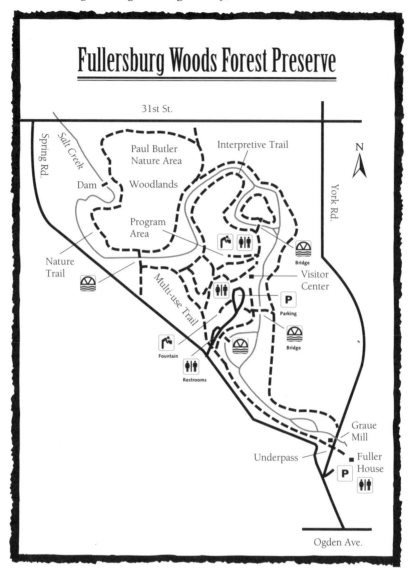

There are connections to the 1.3-miles of interpretive trail and the .75-mile nature trail through the Paul Butler Nature Area in the northwest section of the preserve.

In the 1970s, the creek and the preserve had deteriorated; the creek from the dumping of sewage and other wastes, the preserve from over use by picnickers and other visitors. Through improved sewage treatment and the Forest Preserve District's restoration efforts, the situation is much improved today. The water is cleaner, attracting numerous wildlife including one of North America's most beautiful ducks, the wood duck. The male of this species has a long slick-backed crest and sports an iridescent green, white, and red face pattern. Unlike most duck species, wood ducks fly agilely through the woods and nest in tree cavities. When the young are less than a day old, the mother calls to them from the ground and they tumble free-fall style to be led to the water for their first swim.

Bicycles are restricted from the narrow .3-mile Wildflower Trail and the .8-mile trail through the Paul Butler Nature Area. Lock your bike at the rack near the Visitor Center and take a short hike. In late April through early June, you'll see many native flowers blooming on the Wildflower Trail which starts just to the west of the Visitor Center. On a September visit, the wind unleashed a barrage of acorns from the stately oaks along the way.

The 1.3-mile Interpretive Trail runs along the creek, through woods

Forest Preserve District of DuPage County

Winter in Fullersburg Woods Forest Preserve.

and prairies, and over the bridge to a good-sized island in Salt Creek.
During dry periods, when the water level is low, one branch of Salt
Creek dries up. I guess that makes it a part-time island. You'll find
signs explaining the natural history of the area along the trails. For
example, Salt Creek was named after a farmer's mishap many years
ago. His wagon loaded with salt barrels got stuck in the water.
Overnight much of the salt washed into the creek and thus his little
misadventure lives on.

Just north of the parking area at the Fullersburg Woods Preserve
entrance on Spring Road is the environmental education center.
A 30-minute narrated slide show is available covering the natural
history of DuPage County. Here you can also see an exhibit describing
the woolly mammoth and the Native Americans that hunted him.
Woolly mammoth bones found at Blackwell Forest Preserve in 1977
are on display. Next door at the Visitor Center is a living marsh
exhibit featuring native plants and animals. Nature programs are
offered throughout the year. There are picnic tables, drinking water, a
public phone, and restrooms near the Visitor Center. There are also
restrooms at the Graue Mill parking area. The preserve is open for
cross-country skiing in winter.

Waterfall Glen Forest Preserve

A nearly pristine environment, Waterfall Glen encircles the Argonne National Laboratory in the southeastern part of the county. I-55 runs along the northern border and Route 83 near the eastern side. South of the forest preserve on Route 83, one encounters the conflux of the Santa Fe Railroad tracks, the Des Plaines River, the Chicago Sanitary and Ship Canal, the remnants of the historic I & M Canal, and two huge auto junk yards. With all this nearby "civilization", it's hard to imagine much of an outdoors experience. But once on the 9.5-mile multi-use trail, the outside world is completely forgotten. This is one of the county's most ecologically and scenically diverse areas. You'll find hilly ravines, rock outcroppings, two waterfalls, and bluffs overlooking the Des Plaines River Valley.

Living in this 2,470-acre ring of wilderness are 75 percent of all plant species found in DuPage County. Ten endangered plants and 71 plants of special concern grow here. Scientists recently discovered the federally-endangered emerald dragonfly on the preserve.

There's so much to observe. On a hot humid

Waterfall Glen Forest Preserve

N

I-55

Trailhead

P — Parking
🚰 — Fountain
🚻 — Restrooms

91st St.

Cass Ave.

Westgate Rd.

Linkage Trail   Northgate Rd.

Argonne
National
Laboratory

Linkage
Trail

Rocky Glen &
Waterfall Area   Bluff Rd.

*Sawmill
Creek*

Education Camp

P — Parking
🚰 — Fountain
🚻 — Restrooms

Poverty Prairie

Model Airfield   Signal Hill

gravel road

Poverty
Savanna   Overlook   Old Lincoln
Park Nursery

secondary trail

Des Plaines River

CAUTION
Lemont Police
Shooting Range

Illinois & Michigan Canal National Heritage Corridor (Future Centennial Trail) summer evening, for instance, you might hear the call of the gray tree frog, a tiny woodland amphibian that breeds in marsh areas, then retreats to a woodland habitat for the summer's remainder.

Waterfall Glen is truly one of my favorites!

How to get there:

Take the Argonne National Laboratory/Cass Avenue exit (#273A) off I-55 heading south on Cass. Or take 91st Street 1.4 miles west of Route 83 to Cass Avenue heading north. Turn west at the "Argonne National Laboratory Visitors" sign. Follow the sign to the Waterfall Glen "Ski Equestrian Trailhead" parking area.

In addition to the main trail, there are many mowed turf trails, dirt paths, fire lanes, and service roads throughout the preserve offering miles of somewhat rugged pathways. These are often unmarked and largely unmapped. So if you venture off on the side trails, be sure to bring a map and compass. Also bicyclists are prohibited from the trails that are less than 8 feet wide.

We describe the 9.5-mile multi-purpose trail which consists mostly of crushed limestone surface. On the south and east sides of the preserve, you will find sections of the main trail to be a mixture of packed earth, mowed turf, and narrow rock paths. Follow the trail markers at each intersection to help stay on the main trail. But, as mentioned above, a compass would be handy in case you miss a marker as I did while on the dirt trail on the east side. In 1995, a crushed limestone surface will be installed on the rest of the main trail.

Following is a description heading west. The trail markers point out the main trail in both directions. You'll find water and restrooms at the trailhead. It's a good idea to partake since the next water fountain or restroom is 3/4 of the way around the preserve at the Outdoor Education Camp area.

The Waterfall Glen trail, as well as being fairly long is also by far the most hilly of any preserve or park in the county. If you are cycling, a mountain bike is preferable. There are some rough areas, washouts, and loose gravel on the parts of the trail that are not 8-foot wide crushed limestone surfaced. I did, however, make it around on

Waterfall Glen Forest Preserve

my road bike three times without a problem. The trail leads mostly through beautiful woods of majestic oak and beech trees. Tall pines planted many years ago line the trail.

At 1.9 miles out, you'll come to Westgate Road and an employee entrance into Argonne. This research facility is funded by the U. S. Government for the physical, biomedical, and environmental sciences. Head right (west) on or along Westgate Road for .4 mile. The trail picks up again on the other side of the road. At 3.3 miles out is a large slough- a good place to watch wood ducks sitting on the half-submerged tree limbs or searching for dinner underwater.

At 3.7 miles, you'll come to a rock road crossing (South Bluff Road). Head right (south) on the rock road for .1 mile. The trail resumes across the road next to a model airfield. On your left is the 80-acre Poverty Prairie named for the poverty oat grass that grows in this prairie along with mountain mint and pussytoes. To the right is the 200-acre Poverty Savannah with stately burr oaks rising above the tickle grass and yellow foxglove. Stay on the trail. The Forest Preserve District brochure advises caution since the Lemont Police Department shooting range is south of the savanna. Near present day Lemont, a French trader named DuPage, for whom the county is named, bartered with the Potowatami for furs.

At 4.7 miles out, the main trail climbs a hill to a "T" intersection. To the right along a service road is an information signpost and picnic table. You are now standing on top of a limestone bluff overlooking the Des Plaines River valley to the south. There is a nice scenic view from this spot. In the late 19th and early 20th centuries, limestone quarries flourished in the river valley. You have most likely seen one of the buildings made from this limestone, the Chicago Water Tower on Michigan Avenue. In the early spring or winter, you can see the Des Plaines River below. In 1673, Louis Joliet and Father Marquette canoed by this area during their explorations. An unimproved secondary trail heads west/right out to South Bluff Road. To stay on the main trail take the crushed limestone path to the left down the hill to the Santa Fe Railroad track.

You will pass by concrete walls and shells of buildings, remnants from the Lincoln Park Nursery. Plants were grown here and shipped, along with black topsoil, to Lincoln Park in Chicago. Take the service road left (northeast) for a short distance at 5.4 miles. Follow the trail marker across the service road and take the narrow path up a hill. Here the trail surface is mostly packed earth with gravel in spots.

I suggest walking your bike down the loose gravel path leading to a bridge over Saw Mill Creek 5.9 miles out. From 1860 to 1880, the Ward brothers operated a sawmill near here. To the east is Signal Hill where Native Americans communicated via smoke signals.

As you head back north, you'll come to the Rocky Glen and Waterfall area. A high bluff overlooks the creek below and offers a beautiful view at 6.3 miles out. But don't get too close to the edge—it's a long drop to the creekbed below. After you pass the information signpost, take the first side trail to your left down to the waterfall, which was built by the Civilian Conservation Corps in the 1930s. Note the trail is not open for bike riding. In dry periods, the water flow is only a trickle. But in the spring after a heavy rain, you can enjoy hearing the bubbling brook below the waterfall.

At 6.7 miles out, the main trail passes through the Outdoor Education Camp parking area off of Bluff Road. Here you'll find rest-rooms, drinking water, and a guard residence. The trail resumes on the northeast side of the parking area just before the guard residence. For the next 1.2 miles the trail is a combination of a narrow rock path, mowed turf, and dirt tracks. An 8-foot wide limestone surface will be added in 1995. Cross over Bluff Road at 6.9 miles and continue north.

At 7.9 miles, the crushed limestone surface resumes. An information signpost at 8.3 miles out describes the "still hunting" technique used by Native Americans. Sit quietly and patiently, blend in with the environment, watch, and listen. You will probably observe many animals visiting the nearby lake. The pine trees lining the far shore make this a picturesque spot.

As you head back west to complete the circle, you'll cross four more roads over the last mile of the trail at the forest preserve maintenance center, 91st Street, Cass Road, and Northgate Road.

In the winter, the multi-use trail is open for cross-country skiing. Since the main trail is quite hilly and long, beginners may want to start out with a flatter trail at one of the many other sites described in this guidebook. For the more accomplished skier, the trails here are a real delight. The Norsk Nordic Ski Patrol offers assistance to skiers along the way.

Waterfall Glen Forest Preserve offers one of the most challenging and beautiful trails in DuPage County.

Greenway Interconnecting Trails

For those of you who have read our Lake County guidebook, you may note that some of the following is a repeat, but keep reading to learn about exciting plans for new trails in DuPage County and beyond.

For the beginner hiker or biker, 1, 2, or 5-mile trails are sufficient for getting exercise while enjoying nature. But over time many of us want to push on to adventures of longer distances over different paths and trails. Also hikers and bikers want to try new trails and pathways.

In DuPage County, the rest of Chicagoland, and nationwide, significant progress is being made to interconnect existing park, forest preserve, and other trails. The term greenway is being used to identify a corridor of open land such as an old railroad or utility right-of-way or a waterway that can provide transport for people and/or wildlife while restoring or preserving the natural environment. Often the greenway contains a trail or pathway. The Illinois Prairie

Path (IPP) is a nationally renowned example of a greenway trail.

Greenways provide transportation for not only humans but also for wildlife and plant seedlings. They preserve and protect water and air quality and animal life as well as provide recreational opportunities and self-propelled commuting. Greenway initiatives in Boston, New York, Seattle, and other metropolitan areas have been very successful in linking together existing parks, forests, and trails. Given the high cost of land acquisition and the scarcity of available public funds, greenways are also proving to be the most cost-effective way to provide access to open space. Old railroad right-of-ways, river floodplains, utility right-of-ways, and community developments provide opportunities for the creation of new greenways. Often the trail is surrounded by residential neighborhoods, farms, or other development. You may be able to use a greenway trail to visit a park or forest preserve on your bike rather than in your car. These linear park trails are typically much safer than the highways since contending with horses or bicycles is less risky than dealing with cars, buses, and trucks.

The purpose of this section is to describe some of the activities underway to provide significantly more such trails in the near future within DuPage County and to interconnect with trails originating in the surrounding counties. The Northeastern Illinois Planning Commission (NIPC) is partnering with the Chicago-based Openlands Project to help put in place an interconnected set of trails in the Chicago area that will someday cover 1,000 miles over the six-county Chicago area. There are already over 400 miles of such greenways. In five years it may be possible to make a 200-mile loop throughout Chicagoland to Wisconsin and back with most of the trip on dedicated off-road greenway trails. NIPC and Openlands Project, working with six county forest preserve districts, local communities, and other organizations, have developed an exciting vision of interconnected trails in the Chicago area.

The Northeastern Illinois Regional Greenways Plan was released in May 1993 with this purpose: " The Greenways Plan creates a vision of an interconnected regionwide network of linear open spaces that will provide benefits to northeastern Illinois—environmental, recreational,

economic, aesthetic, and even transportation via trails or waterways."
The plan encompasses Cook, DuPage, Kane, Lake, McHenry, and
Will Counties. Greenway opportunities and priorities for development are laid out. The existing greenway network provides an
excellent starting point including the major waterways (Chicago,
Des Plaines, DuPage, and Fox Rivers), the Lake Michigan shoreline,
old railroad routes (the Illinois Prairie Path, the Great Western Trail
in DeKalb, Kane and DuPage Counties, the North Shore Path in Lake
County, and the Virgil Gilman Trail in Kane County) and even old
canals such as the Illinois and Michigan Canal National Heritage
Corridor.

Focusing on the DuPage County portion, 180 miles of primary
trails are envisioned with more greenways in the central and western
sections. Linking these arteries with a forest preserve trail or local
municipal trail systems such as Oak Brook or Wheaton's pathways
will provide an exciting and enjoyable network of trails criss-crossing
DuPage County and interconnecting with the surrounding counties.

**The Northeastern Illinois Greenways Plan identified the
following top priorities in DuPage County:**

1) Complete the Centennial Trail in the southeastern part of the
county to link with the longer Cook and Will County segments of the
trail. In total, the Centennial Trial will run 20 miles from the Des
Plaines River Trail in Summit to Lockport in Will County. This could
also provide access from Waterfall Glen Forest Preserve to the Cook
County Palos Preserves. (By the end of 1996, 14 miles of the trail will
be completed in Cook, DuPage, and northeastern Will Counties).

2) Preserve more greenway property along the East Branch of the
DuPage River. Develop trails interconnecting Hidden Valley Forest
Preserve, The Morton Arboretum, and Danada/Herrick Lake Forest
Preserves.

3) Complete the Geneva Spur of the IPP. Insure no interruptions
due to road construction. This should be completed by the time you
read this guidebook.

4) Restore Salt Creek as a greenway. Develop a 38-mile Salt Creek
Greenway Trail from the Ned Brown Forest Preserve in Cook County
south through DuPage County and then east to Cook County's exist-

ing 7-mile Salt Creek Trail and on to the Chicago Portage National Historic Site.

5) Acquire additional land along the West Branch of the DuPage River. Extend and interconnect trails from Mallard Lake in the north to the Naperville Riverwalk.

Some specific greenway trail projects planned for the future are as follows:

• Greenway trail between Songbird Slough and Wood Dale Grove Forest Preserves.

• Trail between Churchill Woods and Hidden Lake Forest Preserves.

• Trail from Herrick Lake/Danada Forest Preserves along the northern border of The Morton Arboretum to Hidden Lake Forest Preserve.

• Path connecting Blackwell Forest Preserve with the Aurora Branch of the IPP. (Planned for 1995 completion.)

• Trail from McDowell Grove Forest Preserve to Blackwell Forest Preserve and the Aurora Branch of the IPP.

• Trail from McDowell Grove Forest Preserve to Naperville's Burlington and Pioneer Parks.

• Pratt's Wayne Woods connection to Mallard Lake/West Branch/ Timber Ridge Forest Preserves.

• West DuPage Woods/Winfield Mounds/Timber Ridge Forest Preserves trail to Blackwell Forest Preserve and the Aurora Branch of the IPP.

• Completion of the Great Western Trail to Villa Park including a bridge over I-355 (design work underway).

• Winfield Creek Greenway—connecting the Wheaton EcoBelt with the Great Western Trail and the Aurora Branch of the Illinois Prairie Path. 2.8 miles of additional trail are planned.

• Extension of the Virgil Gilman Trail into DuPage County along Waubansee Creek.

Regional Trail

Here is a good example of an evolving greenway trail that you can hike or bike today. In several sections of this guidebook, the Regional Trail was mentioned. Today you will find a multi-use Regional Trail in

Blackwell, Herrick Lake, and Danada Forest Preserves. With the above mentioned greenway projects, this trail will someday be extended north to Mallard Lake Forest Preserve, south to Naperville, and east to Hidden Lake Forest Preserve covering more than 25 miles of greenways.

At the time of writing, the Regional Trail western trailhead is at the northern border of Blackwell Forest Preserve at Gary's Mill Road. Head southeast to the Blackwell main entrance. In 1995, a new .4-mile trail will be added in Blackwell along the north side of Butterfield Road extending to the Aurora Branch of the Illinois Prairie Path at Winfield Road. Head northeast on the IPP to Atten Park at Weisbrook Road. Turn back south and proceed on the sidewalk next to Weisbrook Road for .5 mile to the Herrick Lake Forest Preserve trail entrance at Butterfield Road. Head south and east to Danada Forest Preserve to the eastern trailhead. When you put it all together you have a 22-mile roundtrip through a variety of natural environments with most of the trip on off-road crushed limestone trail.

Greenways Involvement

Many DuPage County agencies are planning and implementing greenways. These include the Forest Preserve District of DuPage County, the DuPage County Division of Transportation, the Conservation Foundation of DuPage County, The Illinois Prairie Path corporation, the Illinois Department of Conservation, and the following communities:

Aurora	Elmhurst	Oak Brook
Bartlett	Glen Ellyn	Warrenville
Bolingbrook	Hinsdale	West Chicago
Burr Ridge	Lisle	Wheaton
Carol Stream	Lombard	Willowbrook
Downers Grove	Naperville	Woodbridge

NIPC and the Openlands Project provide an excellent vision and framework but community and county governments, regional agencies and organizations, federal and state governments, and private sector corporations, landowners, and interested individuals must play a role in making the plan work. Voice your areas of interest if you'd like to be involved in making the Chicagoland Greenways network happen. For more information call NIPC at 312-454-0400 and/or Openlands Project at 312-427-4256.

Interconnecting Trails in Nearby Counties

Greenway trails in nearby counties offer opportunities for extended bike rides and hikes. Some interconnections are already in place, such as the Fox River Trail in Kane County and farther north the southern section of the Prairie Trail in McHenry County.

• **Fox River Trail System**—This 35-mile asphalt surfaced pathway runs along the picturesque Fox River from Aurora to Algonquin and the McHenry County border. There are four connections with the Illinois Prairie Path as described in Section 1. You will find many communities, forest preserves, museums, and other points of interest along the way. This trail system is well maintained and is one of the most popular in the Chicago area. Call the Kane County Forest Preserve at 708-232-5980 for more information.

• **Prairie Trail**—Built on an old railroad right-of-way, 4.7 miles of asphalt surfaced pathway run through prairie and wetland areas in southeastern McHenry County. The trail can be reached from the IPP via the Fox River Trail. In late 1995 or 1996, this southern section of the Prairie Trail will be connected with an already existing northern portion to offer a 24-mile trail system extending the length of McHenry County to the Wisconsin border. Call the McHenry County Conservation District at 815-678-4431 for more information.

• **Great Western Trail**—A 17-mile crushed limestone trail runs from the west side of St. Charles in Kane County to Sycamore in De-Kalb County. This rails-to-trails conversion crosses streams and wetlands. A 3.5-mile addition is being planned to extend the Great Western Trail eastward to connect with the Fox River Trail. Call the Kane County Forest Preserve District at 708-232-1242 for more information.

• **Virgil Gilman Trail**—An 11-mile nature trail extends from Kane County's southern border at Route 30 through Aurora and west to the Bliss Woods Forest Preserve. Along the way, the trail crosses the Fox

River and Waubansee Creek. An addition scheduled for 1995 will extend the pathway to the Waubansee Community College campus. Also a pathway along the river connecting the Fox River Trail with the Virgil Gilman Trail has recently been funded and will be constructed in the near future. Call the Fox Valley Park District at 708-897-0516 or the Kane County Forest Preserve District at 708-232-5980 for more information.

Beyond Chicagoland

In the introduction to his book, *Greenways for America*, Charles E. Little describes the greenway initiatives as a "remarkable citizen-led movement to get us out of our cars and into the landscape—on paths and trails through corridors of green that can link city to country and people to nature from one end of America to the other." Little traces the origins of greenways back to architects such as Fredrich Law Olmsted, creator of Central Park in New York City. He describes examples both new and old from the Big Sur in California to the Illinois and Michigan Canal National Heritage Corridor to the Hudson River Valley Greenway in New York. The book is an excellent primer for those interested in furthering the development and interconnection of greenways.

The National Park Service, the American Hiking Society, and a coalition of individuals and many trail support organizations are partnering in an effort called "Trails for All Americans—The National Trails Agenda Project." This effort began in 1988 when the President's Commission on American Outdoors recommended the development of a nationwide network of hiking and jogging trails, bikeways, and bridle paths similar to the U. S. Interstate Highway System. It is envisioned that there would be major backbone interstate trails with state, county, and local community trails and interconnecting paths. The hope is that most Americans would live within 15 minutes of a path that could access this national network.

Eight National Scenic and nine Historic Trails provide the major backbone network. Two examples are described below:

• **The Appalachian National Scenic Trail**—a completed 2,144-mile trail through the Appalachian Mountains from Katahdin, Maine to Springer Mountain, Georgia.

• **The Trail of Tears National Historic Trail**—follows the two routes used to move 16,000 Cherokee Indians from Tennessee to Oklahoma, in 1838 and 1839. The water route covers 1,226 miles on the Tennessee, Ohio, Mississippi, and Arkansas Rivers. The 826-mile land route starts in Tennessee, crosses through Kentucky, the southern tip of Illinois, and then Missouri before the sad saga reaches its end in Oklahoma. Development of the entire trail plan has not yet been completed.

While no National Scenic or Historic Trail runs through DuPage County, there is a statewide effort underway to construct a Grand Illinois Trail which will run from the Chicago area to the Mississippi River and back passing through 16 counties along the way. Much of this vast trail system is already in place. (See Section 25 for more information.)

The Grand Illinois Trail

So you say you want to take a really long hike or bike ride! The Illinois Department of Conservation (IDOC) is partnering with many other agencies and organizations to develop one nearby. The Grand Illinois Trail will be a 474-mile circular loop through 16 counties from the western suburbs of Chicago to the Mississippi River and back. Starting at the Chicago Portage in Summit, the trail will use existing trail systems where available as it traverses the state to the Mississippi. Running north along the river the trail will follow the Great River Road corridor to Galena, and then head back to Chicagoland through the counties bordering Wisconsin. Camping and lodging is available along the way. Hikers and bicyclists will be able to see parts of the state they probably have never visited before. Trail enthusiasts will be able to enjoy nearby adventure vacations taking on the entire trail in a single effort or (more likely) completing one segment at a time.

The DuPage County portion is already in place with the Illinois Prairie Path. Other nearby existing trails will include segments of the Grand Illinois such as the Illinois and Michigan Canal State Trail, the Fox River Trail, and the McHenry County Prairie Trail. In fact, 154 miles of off-road trail are already in place. Projects totaling 150 miles are funded and programmed for construction, 37.5 miles of the trail route will use lightly traveled local roads and streets, and 132 miles are proposed for development. The table shows the status of each segment of the Grand Illinois Trail. While it will take some time and a major effort by the involved agencies to construct, the Grand Illinois Trail will be an outstanding asset to trail users as well as the communities along the way.

The "Illinois State Trails Plan" published by IDOC in 1994 describes plans for the Grand Illinois as well as many other trails. If you are interested in finding out more, call IDOC Division of Planning at 217-782-3715.

The Grand Illinois Trail

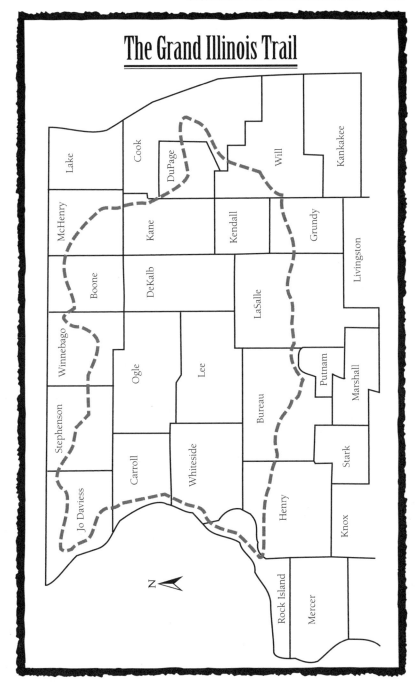

The Grand Illinois Trail

Trail Segment	From-To	# Miles	Existing Off-Road Trails	Existing Streets and Roads	Funded and Programmed for Construction	Proposed
1) Centennial Trail	Summit-Lockport	20	3	1	12.5	3.5
2) Lockport Historical Trail, Joliet Heritage Trail, and local streets	Lockport-Joliet	9	2	2.5	4.5	-
3) I & M Canal State Trail	Joliet-LaSalle	61.8	55.2	-	6.6	-
4) LaSalle-Bureau Junction	LaSalle-Bureau Junction	18.5	-	-	-	18.5
5) Hennepin Canal State Trail	Bureau Junction-Green Rock	75	3	-	72	-
6) Green Rock-East Moline	Green Rock-East Moline	10	-	-	-	10
7) Great River Trail	East Moline-Savanna	65	22	34	6.5	2.5
8) Savanna-Galena-Freeport	Savanna-Freeport	78.7	-	-	-	78.7

Trail Segment	From-To	# Miles	Existing Off-Road Trails	Existing Streets and Roads	Funded and Programmed for Construction	Proposed
9) Pecatonica Prairie Path	Freeport-Rockford	26	21*	-	-	5
10) Rockford Area Trails	Rockford-Roscoe	20	6	-	10	4
11) Stone Bridge Trail Long Prairie Trail	Roscoe-Boone/ McHenry County Line	21	7	-	12	2
12) McHenry County including the Prairie Trail	Boone County Line-Algonquin	28	5.7	-	22.3	-
13) Fox River Trail	Algonquin-Elgin	5.7	5.7	-	-	-
14) Illinois Prairie Path	Elgin-Maywood	27.5	23.5	-	4*	-
15) Des Plaines River Trail	Maywood-Summit	8	-	-	-	8
Total		474.2	154.1	37.5	150.4	132.2

*Existing trail but needs improvement

Appendices

Nearby Attractions

DUPAGE CONVENTION & VISITORS BUREAU
2001 Butterfield Road, Suite 1320, Downers Grove, IL 60515
1-800-232-0502   708-241-0002

Participants with the DuPage Convention & Visitors Bureau
are listed on the following pages 147 to 150.

Accommodations:

Best Western Ambassador Inn
669 Pasquinelli Drive, Westmont 60559
(708) 323-1515   (800) 528-1234

Best Western Four Seasons Motel
656 Taft Avenue, Glen Ellyn 60137
(708) 469-8500   (800) 528-1234

Best Western Inn of Burr Ridge
300 S. Frontage Road, Burr Ridge 60521
(708) 325-2900   (800) 325-0267

Budgetel Inn Willowbrook
855 W. 79th Street, Willowbrook 60521
(708) 654-0077   (800) 428-3438

ClubHouse Inn of Westmont
630 Pasquinelli Drive, Westmont 60559
(708) 920-2200   (800) CLUB-INN

Comfort Inn Aurora
4005 Gabrielle Lane, Aurora 60504
(708) 820-3400   (800) 221-2222

Comfort Inn Downers Grove
3010 Finley Road, Downers Grove 60515
(708) 515-1500   (800) 221-2222

Comfort Suites Oakbrook Terrace
17W445 Roosevelt Road,
Oakbrook Terrace 60181
(708) 916-1000   (800) 221-2222

Drake OakBrook Hotel
2301 York Road, Oak Brook 60521
(708) 574-5700   (800) 235-2230

Embassy Suites Hotel
707 E. Butterfield Road, Lombard 60148
(708) 969-7500   (800) EMBASSY

Exel Inn of Naperville
1585 Naperville/Wheaton Road,
Naperville 60563
(708) 357-0022   (800) 356-8013

Fairfield Inn by Marriott
820 W. 79th Street, Willowbrook 60521
(708) 789-6300   (800) 228-2800

Hampton Inn Lombard
222 E. 22nd Street, Lombard 60148
(708) 916-9000   (800) 426-7866

Harrison House Bed & Breakfast
26 N. Eagle Street, Naperville 60540
(708) 420-1117

The Herrington
15 S. River Lane, Geneva 60134
(708) 208-7433

Hickory Ridge Conference Centre
1195 Summerhill Drive, Lisle 60532
(708) 971-5040   (800) 225-4722

Hilton-Lisle/Naperville
3003 Corporate West Drive, Lisle 60532
(708) 505-0900   (800) 800-HILTONS

Hilton Suites
10 Drury Lane, Oakbrook Terrace 60181
(708) 941-0100   (800) HILTONS 1

Holiday Inn Carol Stream
150 S. Gary Avenue, Carol Stream 60188
(708) 665-3000   (800) 800-6509

Holiday Inn Chicago-Elmhurst
624 N. York Road, Elmhurst 60126
(708) 279-1100   (800) HOLIDAY

Holiday Inn Express
3031 Finley Road, Downers Grove 60515
(708) 810-9500   (800) HOLIDAY

Holiday Inn Glen Ellyn
1250 Roosevelt Road, Glen Ellyn 60137
(708) 629-6000   (800) HOLIDAY

Holiday Inn Naperville
1801 Naper Boulevard, Naperville 60563
(708) 505-4900   (800) HOLIDAY

Holiday Inn Willowbrook
7800 Kingery Drive, Willowbrook 60521
(708) 325-6400   (800) HOLIDAY

Hyatt Lisle
1400 Corporetum Drive, Lisle 60532
(708) 852-1234   (800) 233-1234

Hyatt Regency Oak Brook
1909 Spring Road, Oak Brook 60521
(708) 573-1234   (800) 233-1234

Indian Lakes Resort
250 W. Schick Road, Bloomingdale 60108
(708) 529-0200   (800) 334-3417

La Quinta Motor Inn
1S666 Midwest Road, Oakbrook Terrace
60181
(708) 495-4600   (800) 531-5900

Marriott Suites Downers Grove
1500 Opus Place, Downers Grove 60515
(708) 852-1500   (800) 228-9290

Motel 6 Villa Park
10 W. Roosevelt Road, Villa Park 60181
(708) 941-9100

Nordic Hills Resort & Conference Center
Route 53 & Nordic Road, Itasca 60143
(708) 773-2750   (800) 334-3417

Oak Brook Hills Hotel & Resort
3500 Midwest Road, Oak Brook 60522-6010
(708) 850-5555   (800) 445-3315

Oak Brook Marriott Hotel
1401 W. 22nd Street, Oak Brook 60521
(708) 573-8555   (800) 228-9290

Pheasant Run Resort & Convention Center
4051 E. Main Street, St. Charles 60174
(708) 584-6300

Radisson Hotel Lisle-Naperville
3000 Warrenville Avenue, Lisle 60532
(708) 505-1000   (800) 333-3333

Radisson Suite Hotel-Downers Grove
2111 Butterfield Road, Downers Grove
60515
(708) 971-2000   (800) 333-3333

Red Roof Inn Downers Grove
1113 Butterfield Road, Downers Grove
60515
(708) 963-4205   (800) THE ROOF

Red Roof Inn Naperville
1698 W. Diehl Road, Naperville 60563
(708) 369-2500   (800) THE ROOF

Red Roof Inn Willowbrook
7535 Kingery Highway, Willowbrook
60521
(708) 323-8811   (800) THE ROOF

Residence Inn by Marriott
2001 Highland Avenue, Lombard 60148
(708) 629-7800   (800) 331-3131

Stouffer Renaissance Oak Brook Hotel
2100 Spring Road, Oak Brook 60521
(708) 573-2800   (800) HOTELS 1

Attractions:

Argonne National Laboratory
9700 S. Cass Avenue, Argonne 60439
(708) 252-5562

Billy Graham Center Museum
500 E. College Avenue, Wheaton 60187
(708) 752-5909

Brookfield Zoo
1st Avenue and 31st Street, Brookfield
60513
(708) 485-0263

Cantigny
1S151 Winfield Road, Wheaton, 60187
(708) 668-5161

Drury Lane Theatre
100 Drury Lane, Oakbrook Terrace 60181
(708) 530-8300

DuPage Children's Museum
1777 S. Blanchard Road, Wheaton 60187
(708) 260-9960

DuPage County Historical Museum
102 E. Wesley Street, Wheaton 60187
(708) 682-7343

Elmhurst Art Museum
130 W. Madison Street, Elmhurst 60126
(708) 834-0202

Elmhurst Historical Museum
120 E. Park Avenue, Elmhurst 60126
(708) 833-1457

Empress River Casino
2300 Empress Drive, Joliet 60436
(815) 744-1671   (800)

Enchanted Castle Restaurant &
Entertainment Center
1103 S. Main Street, Lombard 60148
(708) 953-7860

Fermi National Accelerator Laboratory
Kirk & Pine Streets, Batavia 60510
(708) 840-3351

Frank Lloyd Wright Home & Studio
951 Chicago Avenue, Oak Park 60302
(708) 848-1500

Graue Mill & Museum
York Road north of Ogden Avenue, Oak
Brook 60521
(708) 655-2090

Harrah's Casino Joliet
150 N. Scott Street, Joliet 60431
(815) 740-7800

Here's Chicago
163 E. Pearson, Chicago 60611
(312) 467-7114

Hollywood Casino
49 W. Galena Boulevard, Aurora 60506
(708) 801-7000

Lisle Station Park
919 Burlington Avenue, Lisle 60532
(708) 968-2747

Lizzadro Museum of Lapidary Art
220 Cottage Hill, Elmhurst 60126
(708) 833-1616

Lombard Historical Society Museum
23 W. Maple, Lombard 60148
(708) 629-1885

Lombard Park District
150 S. Park Avenue, Lombard 60148
(708) 620-7322

The Morton Arboretum
Rte. 53, Lisle 60532
(708) 968-0074

Naper Settlement Museum Village
201 W. Porter Avenue, Naperville 60563
(708) 420-6010

National Shrine of St. Therese & Museum
8501 Bailey Road, Darien 60561
(708) 969-5050

Paramount Arts Centre
23 E. Galena Boulevard, Aurora 60506
(708) 896-6666

Prairie Landing Golf Course
2325 Longest Drive, West Chicago 60186
(708) 208-7600

Robert Crown Center for Health Education
21 Salt Creek Lane, Hinsdale 60521
(708) 325-1900

SciTech
18 W. Benton, Aurora 60506
(708) 859-8112

Seven Bridges Golf Course
3750 Hobson Road, Woodridge 60517
(708)

Shark City Billiards & Sports Bar
2240 Bloomingdale Road, Glendale Heights
60139
(708) 893-9346

Spirit of Chicago Harbor Cruises
455 E. Illinois Street, Chicago 606
(312) 836-7888

Stacy's Tavern
557 Geneva Road, Glen Ellyn 60137
(708) 858-8696

Warrenville Historical Society Museum
2S530 Second Street, Warrenville 60555
(708) 393-4215

West Chicago City Museum
132 Main Street, West Chicago 60185
(708) 231-3376

Westmont Park District
55 E. Richmond Street, Westmont 60559
(708) 960-3392

Wheaton History Center
606 N. Main Street, Wheaton 60187
(708) 682-9472

Whirlyball
800 E. Roosevelt Road, Lombard 60148
(708) 932-4800

William L. Gregg Museum
350 W. 59th Street, Westmont 60559
(708) 960-3392

Shopping:

Fox Valley Center
Rte. 59 and New York Avenue, Aurora
60506
(708) 851-7200

Oakbrook Center
22nd Street and Rte. 83, Oak Brook 60521
(708) 573-1300

Stratford Square
Army Trail and Gary Avenue, Bloomingdale
60108
(708) 351-9405

Yorktown Center
Highland Avenue at Butterfield Road,
Lombard 60148
(708) 629-7330

Excursions/Tours:

American Sightseeing Tours-Chicago
27 E. Monroe Street, Chicago 60603
(312) 427-3100

Chicago Gray Line Tours
27 E. Monroe Street, Chicago 60603
(312) 427-3107

Mid-America Charter Lines, Inc.
2513 E. Higgins Road, Elk Grove Village
60007
(708) 437-3709

Nearby Bike Shops

You will find bike shops conveniently located near many of the trails and bike paths described in this guidebook.

A & J's Hillside Cyclery
4049 Washington Boulevard
Hillside, IL 60162
708-544-7200

Addison Cycle Center
514 Lake Street
Addison, IL 60101
708-543-4680

Allen's Schwinn Cyclery
40 East St. Charles Road
Villa Park, IL 60180-2442
708-834-0813

Bicycle Specialties, Inc.
1628 Ogden Avenue
Downers Grove, IL 60515
708-963-4616

Bicycles Etc.
6474 College Road
Lisle, IL 60532
708-369-2453

The Bike Rack
37W610 Campton
Hills Road
St. Charles, IL 60174
708-584-6588

Blazing Saddles
888 West 75th Street
Willowbrook, IL 60521
708-986-2453

Broken Spoke
6330 Woodward Avenue
Downers Grove, IL 60516
708-964-0090

Camelot Bike & Ski
23W458 North Avenue
Carol Stream, IL 60188
708-668-0700

DuPage Cyclery & Fitness
567 South Route 59
Aurora, IL 60504
708-898-8600

**Erewhon Mountain
Outfitter**
1512 North Naper
Naperville, IL 60540
708-955-0030

Fox River Schwinn
19 South Lincolnway
North Aurora, IL 60542
708-897-6200

Glen Ellyn Cyclery
460 Roosevelt
Glen Ellyn, IL 60137
708-858-6400

**Hartley's Cycle
Shoppe Ltd.**
24 West Hinsdale Avenue
Hinsdale, IL 60521
708-323-7156

J & R Cyclery
716 South Main
Lombard, IL, 60148
708-620-1606

Koslow Cycle, Inc.
21W415 North Avenue
Lombard, IL 60148
708-629-4773

Midwest Cyclery
229 West Front Street
Wheaton, IL 60187
708-668-2424

Mill Race Cyclery
11 East State Street
Geneva, IL 60134
708-232-2833

**Naperville Cycling
& Fitness**
1001 East Ogden Avenue
Naperville, IL 60563-8607
708-355-2200

Pedal & Spoke Ltd.
157 South Lincolnway
North Aurora, IL 60542
708-892-1010

**Performance
Bicycle Shop**
484 South Route 59
Suite 104
Naperville, IL 60540
708-983-3010

Prairie Path Schwinn
27W111 Geneva Road
Winfield, IL 60190
708-690-9749

ProBikes & Likes, Inc.
494 Crescent Boulevard
Glen Ellyn, IL 60137
708-858-6665

Spokes
1807 South Washington
Naperville, IL 60565
708-961-8222

Spokes
223 Rice Lake Square
Wheaton, IL 60187
708-690-2050

Stemple's Cycle Center
494 Spring Road
Elmhurst, IL 60126
708-834-1012

Sundance Cycle
160 South Bloomingdale
Road
Bloomingdale, IL 60108
708-980-3136

The Wheel Shop, Inc.
47 East Illinois Avenue
Aurora, IL 60505
708-896-2400

Information provided by the Chicago Area Bicycle Dealers Association

Calendar of Events

Each event is shown under the month typically scheduled. Call to get specific information.

January

    Ice Fishing Tips & Tricks, Songbird Slough
    Forest Preserve District of DuPage County   708-790-4900

February

    Ice Cutting, Kline Creek Farm
    Forest Preserve District of DuPage County   708-790-4900

March

    Maple Syruping, Fullersburg Woods
    & Kline Creek Farm
    Forest Preserve District of DuPage County   708-790-4900

April

    Arbor Day Weekend
    The Morton Arboretum, Lisle   708-719-2465

    Earth Day, Fullersburg Woods
    Forest Preserve District of DuPage County   708-790-4900

    Illinois Prairie Path Spring Cleanup
    (Near Earth Day)   708-752-0120

May

    The Best of the West
    Greater Wheaton Cycle Classic
    (15, 30, and 60 mile bike rides)   708-668-6464

    Lilac Time, Lombard   708-953-6000

    Naperville 10 K Classic   708-717-0500

June

Cream of Wheaton
Wheaton Park District   708-665-4710

DuPage River Sweep
Conservation Foundation of DuPage County   708-682-3505

Elmfest, Elmhurst   708-834-6060

Heritage Festival, Downers Grove   708-964-0300

"Just for Kids" Fishing Derby, Blackwell
Forest Preserve District of DuPage County   708-790-4900

Run for the Animals (5K/10K)
The Cosley Foundation, Wheaton   708-665-5534

Sculpture Show at Cantigny   708-241-0002

July

DuPage County Fair, Wheaton   708-668-6636

Ice Cream Social, Kline Creek Farm
Forest Preserve District of DuPage County   708-790-4900

Melon Metric 32M/62M/100M Bike Tour
Naperville Bicycle Club   708-357-9000
Sandwich, IL   ext. 616

Turn-Of-The-Century Days
Naper Settlement, Naperville   708-420-6010

August

U. S. Pro Criterium Championship Bicycle Races
Downers Grove   708-719-4600

West Fest, Oak Brook Terrace   708-941-8305

Prairie Festival, Illinois Prairie Path
Elmhurst Park District   708-993-8909

September

Autumn Fest
Memorial Park, Wheaton   708-668-2739

Fall Plowing, Kline Creek Farm
Forest Preserve District of DuPage County   708-790-4900

Family Fair
The Morton Arboretum, Lisle   708-719-2465

Pow Wow Days, Westmont   708-654- 2894

St. James Farm Steeplechase Races
St. James Farm, Warrenville   708-46-CHASE

October

Danada Equestrian Fall Festival
Harvest Festival-Kline Creek Farm
Forest Preserve District of DuPage County   708-790-4900

Volunteer Prairie Seed Harvest
Fermilab   708-840-3351

November

Downers Grove Park District Turkey Trot (5K)
Downers Grove   708-963-1300

Dan Gibbons Turkey Trot (5K)
Elmhurst   708-369-1000

Illinois Prairie Path Annual Meeting   708-752-0120

December

Christmas on the Farm-Kline Creek Farm
Forest Preserve District of DuPage County   708-790-4900

Christmas Memories and Candlelight Strolls
Naper Settlement Museum Village
Naperville   708-420-6010

Special Ongoing Activities

Adopt-An-Acre & Parent-A-Tree Programs
Forest Preserve District of DuPage County   708-790-4900

Bike Rides, Field Trips, Bird Hikes,
Work Days scheduled throughout the
year on the Illinois Prairie Path   708-752-0120

Restoration Workdays (September–May)
DuPage Volunteer Stewardship Group   708-246-9561

Organizations

Bicycle Clubs

Chicagoland Bicycle Federation   312-42 PEDAL
343 S. Dearborn, Suite 1017
Chicago, IL 60604

Elmhurst Bicycle Club   708-415-BIKE
P. O. Box 902
Elmhurst, IL 60126

Flyer Bicycle Club   708-443-9840
c/o Ride Safe
P. O. Box 888
Warrenville, IL 60555

League of Illinois Bicyclists   708-433-4075
49 Valley Road
Highland Park, IL 60035

Naperville Bicycle Club   708-357-9000
320 W. Jackson   ext. 616
Naperville, IL 60540

Environmental

Conservation Foundation of DuPage County   708-682-3505
703 Warrenville Road
Wheaton, IL 60187

DuPage Volunteer Stewardship Group   708-246-9561

Fermilab Prairie Project Volunteers   708-840-3351

Forest Preserve District Volunteers   708-790-4900
185 Spring Street,
Glen Ellyn, IL 60137

Partners for the Lincoln Marsh   708-665-5534
Cosley Park

The Nature Conservancy, Illinois Field Office   312-346-8166
8 S. Michigan, Suite 900
Chicago, IL 60603

Sierra Club-River Prairie Group   708-690-4930
506 S. Wabash #505
Chicago, IL 60605

The Morton Arboretum   708-719-2400
Lisle, IL 60532

West Chicago Prairie Stewardship Group   708-393-4715

Willowbrook Wildlife Foundation   708-790-4900
525 Park Boulevard   Ext. 245
Glen Ellyn, IL 60137

Hiking and Walking

American Hiking Society   703-385-3252
P. O. Box 20160
Washington, D. C. 20041

Earth Spirit Walking Club   708-941-7151
2205 Oakland Street
Villa Park, IL 60181

Trails

The Illinois Prairie Path   708-752-0120
P. O. Box 1086
Wheaton, IL 60189

Rails-to-Trails Conservancy   217-789-4782
319 W. Cook Street,
Springfield, IL 62704

Other

DuPage County Historical Museum Association   708-682-7343
102 East Wesley Street
Wheaton, IL 60187

Norsk Nordic Ski Patrol   708-790-3935

Trail Riders of DuPage (TROD)   708-887-8542
5765 Virginia
Clarendon Hills, IL 60514

Bibliography

Books

The Complete Guide to America's National Parks. National Park Foundation. 1992-93 Edition.

Country Walks Near Chicago. Fisher, Alan. Rambler Books. 1987.

DuPage Roots. Thompson, Richard A. DuPage County Historical Society. 1985.

Greenways for America. Little, Charles E. Johns Hopkins University Press. 1990.

Other Publications

State of The Greenways Report. Prepared by Northeastern Illinois Planning Commission and Openlands Project. July, 1994.

The DuPage Conservationist. Quarterly Newsletter of the Forest Preserve District of DuPage County.

The Northestern Illinois Regional Greenways Plan. Developed by the Northeastern Illinois Planning Commission and Openlands Project. May, 1993.

Trails for all Americans—The Report of the National Trails Agenda Project. Submitted by American Trails to the National Park Service. Summer, 1990.

Comments from Our Customers

Your comments related to this guidebook are very much appreciated for our use in improving future issues.

_____

_____

_____

_____

We are also considering publishing other hiking/biking guidebooks. Would you be interested in the following?

	Level of Interest		
	High	**Medium**	**Low**
• Hiking and Biking in Cook County, Illinois	☐	☐	☐
• Hiking and Biking in Kane and McHenry Counties, Illinois	☐	☐	☐
• Hiking and Biking in Indiana's Parks and Forests	☐	☐	☐
• Hiking and Biking in Door County, Wisconsin	☐	☐	☐
• Hiking Made Easy in the Great Smoky Mountain National Park	☐	☐	☐
• Hiking and Biking in Southeastern Wisconsin	☐	☐	☐

We will be happy to include you on our mailing list to announce any upcoming products.

Name _____

Address _____

City, State, Zip Code _____

Thanks for your input.

Order Form

Send _____ copy/copies of Roots & Wings Hiking & Biking guide-books to the following address:

Name _____

Address _____

City, State, Zip Code _____

Please enclose a personal check for the total amount made payable to Roots & Wings, P.O. Box 167, Lake Forest, Illinois, 60045. Thank you for your order!

_____ books @ $10.95 = _____   *Hiking & Biking in*
                                          Lake County, Illinois

_____ books @ $11.95 = _____   *Hiking & Biking in*
                                          DuPage County, Illinois

Subtotal   = _____

Illinois Residents Add
Sales Tax @ 6.5%   = _____

Shipping and Handling   = ___$1.95___

Total   = _____

You may also buy additional copies of these guidebooks at bookstores, bicycle shops, nature stores, and outfitters as well as other merchants throughout Chicagoland.